Letts
gets you through

KS2 ENGLISH
SATs SUCCESS
WORKBOOK

Ages 7–11

KS2
ENGLISH
SATs

WORKBOOK

SHELLEY WELSH

Contents

Grammar and Punctuation

Spelling

Speaking and Listening

SATs Practice Questions

Glossary

Answers

Set in a pull-out booklet in the centre of the book

1 Under the column headings, name as many different **genres** of fiction and non-fiction that you can think of. **(3 marks)**

Fiction	Non-fiction

2 What is the purpose of the **blurb** on the back of a book? **(1 mark)**

3 In which genre of non-fiction are you most likely to find the following? **(1 mark)**

- contents page
- index
- glossary
- illustrations, pictures, tables, graphs and diagrams

4 Look at the front covers of these books. Draw a line to match them up to the appropriate genre. **(4 marks)**

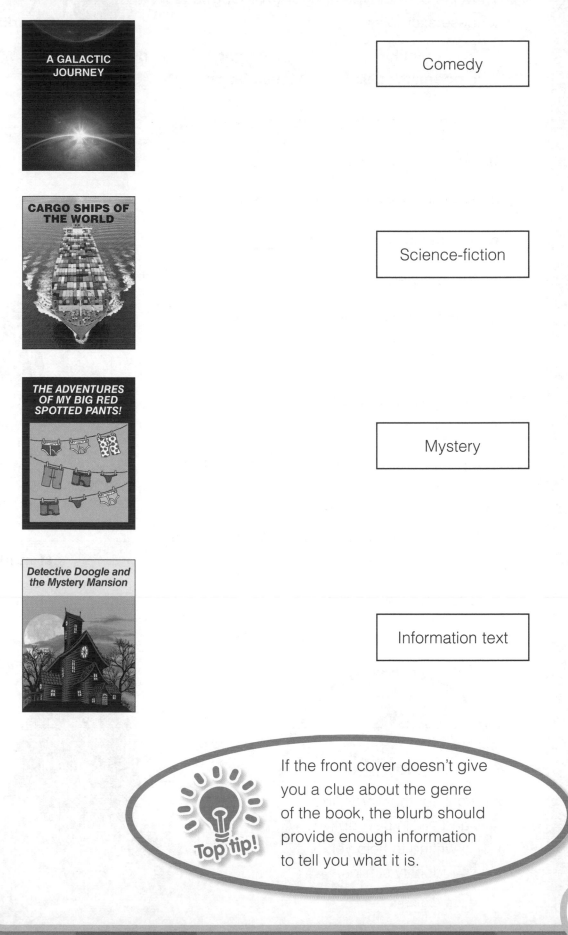

Comedy

Science-fiction

Mystery

Information text

Top tip! If the front cover doesn't give you a clue about the genre of the book, the blurb should provide enough information to tell you what it is.

Total 9

Figurative language

1 Write the correct type of **figurative language** next to these examples.

(6 marks)

simile	metaphor	personification
onomatopoeia	alliteration	assonance

a. Bang, crash, wallop! Dad was cooking again ....

b. Four poor dormice ran across the floor. ....

c. His fingers were as cold as ice. ....

d. The mountains were sleeping giants. ....

e. My feet were blocks of ice. ....

f. Five filthy foxes fled through the fields. ....

Similes

1 Write appropriate **similes** for the following. An example has been done for you.

The princess's skin was as *pale as a milky pearl* ....

a. Her eyes twinkled like .... **(1 mark)**

b. The rain hammered on the roof, as loud as ....

(1 mark)

c. The wind howled like .... **(1 mark)**

d. We charged onto the playing field like ....

(1 mark)

Top tip!

Look for the words 'like' and 'as' in descriptive writing to help you identify similes.

Metaphors

1 Which sentence below uses a **metaphor** to describe 'our last day in Year 6'?
Tick one. **(1 mark)**

   a. Our last day in Year 6 was like a rollercoaster of emotions. ☐

   b. On our last day in Year 6, we went on a rollercoaster. ☐

   c. Our last day in Year 6 was a rollercoaster of emotions. ☐

   d. Our last day in Year 6 was very emotional. ☐

2 The sentences below use similes to compare two things.
Rewrite them, turning the similes into metaphors.

   a. My heart was beating like a carpenter's busy hammer. **(1 mark)**

   ....

   b. The snow on the hills was like a white, fluffy blanket. **(1 mark)**

   ....

   c. My tears were like rushing rivers flooding down my cheeks. **(1 mark)**

   ....

   d. My best friend Ajamil is like a walking dictionary. **(1 mark)**

   ....

Personification

1 Highlight **four** examples of **personification** in the following passage: **(4 marks)**

Soon the two friends entered a clearing where the gnarled and twisted fleshless
fingers of hunched trees brushed the forest floor in the wind. They couldn't afford to
be afraid and there appeared to be a cave further along where they might take refuge.
A sudden gust of wind attacked them from behind so they didn't stop to reconsider.
Cautiously, the children entered the yawning cave which soon consumed them…

2 Write a sentence about a mountain using appropriate personification. **(2 marks)**

....

Total $\frac{}{21}$

Onomatopoeia

1 Underline the examples of **onomatopoeia** in the sentences below.

    a. The horse's hooves clattered across the cobbles.   **(1 mark)**

    b. The bees were buzzing around the flowers.   **(1 mark)**

    c. Click! Dad switched the fairy lights on.   **(1 mark)**

    d. The drink fizzed over the top of my glass.   **(1 mark)**

    e. The rain bubbled in the gutters.   **(1 mark)**

    f. We could hear the leaves rustling in the wind.   **(1 mark)**

2 Write an onomatopoeic word linked to the sounds of these nouns.

    a. water: ....   **(1 mark)**

    b. wind: ....   **(1 mark)**

    c. cow: ....   **(1 mark)**

    d. cat: ....   **(1 mark)**

    e. horn: ....   **(1 mark)**

    f. clock: ....   **(1 mark)**

Top tip! Use figurative language when discussing poems. Knowing and recognising different types of figurative language can help you understand a poem better.

Alliteration

1 Highlight examples of **alliteration** in the following sentences.

   a. The turtles slithered across the soft sand towards the sea.   **(1 mark)**

   b. I dangled dangerously from the death-defying cliff edge.   **(1 mark)**

   c. He held the bloodied blade above the beast's bedraggled body.   **(1 mark)**

   d. Katie cooked cupcakes in her cosy kitchen.   **(1 mark)**

2 Write sentences containing the following words, with at least one example of alliteration. An example has been done for you.

horse: *The hungry horse hurtled down the hill.*

   a. lion   **(1 mark)**

   ....

   b. granny   **(1 mark)**

   ....

   c. prince   **(1 mark)**

   ....

   d. wind   **(1 mark)**

   ....

Assonance

1 Highlight the examples of assonance in the verse below.   **(2 marks)**

Creeping three at a time
The creatures seek shelter
From the whistling wind.
Under the bright night sky,
They hide inside and cry,
Praying for day.

Total — 22

Read the chapter below then answer the questions on the next page.

Chapter 49 *Mortal Chaos* by Matt Dickinson

Fields above Chinchewe village, Malawi, East Africa.

Kamuzu was exhausted. He had spent more than twelve hours wrapped up in a blanket on the small wooden platform which acted as a look-out post, only descending to scare away the baboons or to tend to the little fire he kept for comfort. He kept glancing down to the valley floor, yearning for the sight of Bakili coming along the trail to take over the job.

But there was no sign of his younger brother.

Then he heard a squabble amongst the baboons, followed by silence and then the distinctive crunching of maize stalks. Kamuzu got quickly to his feet, standing on his toes to determine where the raid was happening. Then he hollered loudly, uttering a series of high pitched cries in the hope of scaring the animals as he rushed into the maize with his stick.

Kamuzu rushed through the tall maize, whistling and yelling at the top of his young voice. He could see no more than a couple of metres ahead, but he could hear the sound of the scavengers ripping into the crop and he used the noise to orientate himself.

There.

The baboons were right in front. Kamuzu burst through the maize and slammed his stick hard against the ground just an arm's length from the nearest animal. He could see it was the big one – the alpha male – and normally he would expect the creature to run. But the baboon did not run. In fact it did the very last thing that Kamuzu expected.

The baboon attacked him with its fangs fully bared, rushing beneath Kamuzu's upraised stick and delivering a savage bite to the child's inside thigh.

1 Who is Bakili? **Tick one.** (1 mark)

a baboon ☐ Kamuzu's brother ☐

Kamuzu's friend ☐ Kamuzu's boss ☐

2 What is the meaning of the phrase 'yearning for' in the first paragraph? (1 mark)

....

3 What did the sound of 'distinctive crunching of maize stalks' tell Kamuzu? (1 mark)

....

4 Why did Kamuzu whistle and yell as he went through the maize? (1 mark)

....

5 What word does the author use that describes the baboons as animals that will eat all kinds of things? (1 mark)

....

6 Why could Kamuzu only see a couple of metres in front of him? (1 mark)

....

7 How did the noise of the baboons eating help Kamuzu? (1 mark)

....

8 What is the effect of the way the word *There.* is written? (2 marks)

....

....

9 What do you think 'alpha male' means? (1 mark)

....

10 Why would Kamuzu have been surprised at the baboon's attack? (1 mark)

....

Total $\frac{}{11}$

Read the poem below then answer the questions.

Wind by Ted Hughes

This house has been far out at sea all night,
The woods crashing through darkness, the booming hills,
Winds stampeding the fields under the window
Floundering black astride and blinding wet

Till day rose; then under an orange sky
The hills had new places, and wind wielded
Blade-light, luminous black and emerald,
Flexing like the lens of a mad eye.

At noon I scaled along the house-side as far as
The coal-house door. Once I looked up -
Through the brunt wind that dented the balls of my eyes
The tent of the hills drummed and strained its guyrope,

The fields quivering, the skyline a grimace,
At any second to bang and vanish with a flap;
The wind flung a magpie away and a black-
Back gull bent like an iron bar slowly. The house

Rang like some fine green goblet in the note
That any second would shatter it. Now deep
In chairs, in front of the great fire, we grip
Our hearts and cannot entertain book, thought,

Or each other. We watch the fire blazing,
And feel the roots of the house move, but sit on,
Seeing the window tremble to come in,
Hearing the stones cry out under the horizons.

1 What does the narrator mean when he says the house 'has been far out at sea all night'? **(2 marks)**

....

....

 Remember to scan the poem to find key words and phrases!

2 Look at the table below. In the left-hand column, what are the words in bold being compared to?

Write your answer in the right-hand column.

The first one has been done for you.   **(3 marks)**

Text	What the author is comparing
Winds stampeding the fields under the window	*Winds are being compared to a herd of animals.*
The tent of **the hills** drummed and strained its guyrope	....
The house Rang like some fine green goblet	....
We … feel the roots of **the house** move	....

3 Although the narrator is inside by the fire, what are he and his companion struggling to do?

(1 mark)

....

4 Explain what this simile is telling us.   **(2 marks)**

a black-
Back gull bent like an iron bar slowly.

....

....

5 There is a lot of personification in the poem.

Choose one example and say why you think it is effective.   **(1 mark)**

Example: ....

Why I think it is effective: ....

....

Total $\frac{}{9}$

Read the poem below then answer the questions.

Nettles by Vernon Scannell

My son aged three fell in the nettle bed.
'Bed' seemed a curious name for those green spears,
That regiment of spite behind the shed:
It was no place for rest. With sobs and tears
The boy came seeking comfort and I saw
White blisters beaded on his tender skin.
We soothed him till his pain was not so raw.
At last he offered us a watery grin,
And then I took my billhook, honed the blade
And went outside and slashed in fury with it
Till not a nettle in that fierce parade
Stood upright any more. And then I lit
A funeral pyre to burn the fallen dead,
But in two weeks the busy sun and rain
Had called up tall recruits behind the shed:
My son would often feel sharp wounds again.

❶ Why do you think the poet thought the word 'bed' was a curious name
to describe the place the nettles grew?   **(2 marks)**

....

....

❷ Why did the poet's son come 'seeking comfort'?   **(1 mark)**

....

....

3 What does the verb 'beaded' tell you about the appearance of the boy's skin?

(1 mark)

....

4 Explain what the poet means by a 'watery grin'. **(1 mark)**

....

5 What do you think the poet was doing when he 'honed the blade'? **(1 mark)**

....

6 'The poet over-reacts in the way he deals with the nettles after what happens to his son'. Give evidence from the text to support this viewpoint. **(2 marks)**

....

....

....

7 How do we know the poet hasn't managed to get rid of the nettles from behind the shed? **(1 mark)**

....

....

Top tip! After your first reading, do a second 'skim' read of the text to help you understand it more.

Total $\frac{}{9}$

Read the information text below and answer the questions on the next page.

Pole to Pole

The polar regions are the extremely cold areas found to the far north and south of our planet. They are considered to be among the most inhospitable places on Earth and were the last large areas on Earth to be explored.

The Arctic

The northern polar region is known as the Arctic. This is a huge ocean surrounded by land. The North Pole (the most northerly point on Earth) is in this ocean. However, it is possible to get to the North Pole on foot, because a large proportion of the ocean remains frozen all year round.

During the Arctic winter, the sun never rises and during the summer it never sets, although it remains low in the sky and is therefore very weak.

Although people live on the land at the edge of the Arctic Ocean, they do not live at the North Pole because the ice is floating and moving.

The Antarctic

The Antarctic is the southern polar region and the South Pole can be found here. Unlike the North Pole, the South Pole is completely surrounded by land.

As with the Arctic, the sun never rises during an Antarctic winter and remains close to the horizon during the summer. However, throughout the year the Antarctic remains much colder, partly due to the fact that most of the continent is high above sea level and is covered in thousands of metres of ice, rather than just a few metres as in the Arctic.

There are no native inhabitants on the Antarctic land mass, but special international treaties allow scientists from many countries to live there and undertake valuable research. Much of the information we know about the ozone layer and global warming has come from these scientists.

1 What do you think the word 'inhospitable' means in the opening paragraph? **(1 mark)**

....

2 Where is the North Pole located? **(1 mark)**

....

3 What makes it possible to reach the North Pole on foot? **(1 mark)**

....

4 What prevents people from living at the North Pole? **(1 mark)**

....

5 **Tick** the box to indicate which statements apply to which area. **(4 marks)**

	The Arctic	The Antarctic
Sun does not rise in winter		
Sun is low in the sky in summer		
Most of the continent is high above sea level		
Scientists carry out research there		

6 What makes the Antarctic much colder than the Arctic? **(2 marks)**

....

....

Total $\frac{}{10}$

Read the explanation text below and answer the questions on the next page.

How do camels survive in the desert?

Camels are herbivores: they eat desert vegetation, such as grasses, herbs and leaves. Like all animals, they need water to survive but there isn't a lot of it around in the desert! So how do they manage in extreme temperatures? Camels have several physical characteristics that help them survive in harsh desert conditions.

Where's that water?

Water is rare in the desert but camels have an in-built hydration system; they store fat in the humps on their backs which can be chemically converted to water and energy when necessary. This sustains camels over long distances until they reach the next watering hole (called an oasis); however, in winter they can literally go months without needing to drink.

Did you know?
- Camels hardly ever urinate or sweat.
- Their dung is very dry, allowing Bedouins to use it for fuel.
- A camel can drink up to 32 gallons (46 litres) of water in one 13-minute drinking session!

Ears, nose and eyes

Camels have many adaptations that allow them to live successfully in desert conditions. If a sandstorm blows up, it is vital that the camel doesn't lose its way or damage its eyesight. Their long eyelashes protect their eyes from potentially damaging grains of sand and their nostrils can close to prevent sand going up their noses. Their ears are covered with hair, inside and out, to prevent sand and dust finding its way in. Finally, their thick eyebrows shield their eyes from the fierce desert sun.

Pucker up!

A camel's lips are so thick that they can grasp leaves, spiky plants and other vegetation without losing precious moisture from their tongues or feeling any pain. Once they have swallowed the food, their three stomachs re-digest it multiple times to extract all potential nutrition.

Feet first!

Camels' feet are wide so they can walk on sand more easily; the large surface area means they don't sink into the sand.

1 Tick the box which completes this sentence. **Tick one.** (1 mark)

Camels are herbivores which means they eat:

a. meat ☐

b. fish ☐

c. plants ☐

d. meat and plants ☐

2 What does the author mean by 'an in-built hydration system'? (1 mark)

....

3 Which verb in the second paragraph tells you that the fat in the camel's hump keeps it going for a while? (1 mark)

....

4 Why do you think camels rarely urinate or sweat? (1 mark)

....

5 Give two reasons why camels have thick lips.

a. .... (1 mark)

b. .... (1 mark)

6 What is unusual about a camel's digestive system? (1 mark)

....

7 What do Bedouin tribes use to make their fires? (1 mark)

....

Total — 8

Look at these two adverts and answer the questions on the next page.

A.

RunFaster Trainers!

You'll never buy another brand...

Do you maximise your full potential? You won't if you haven't got **RunFaster** trainers.

- Air-cushioned in-soles
- Rubberised treads
- Fully waterproofed exteriors
- Aerodynamic

World-class athlete, Harry Hurdle, wouldn't be seen in anything else.

"**RunFaster** trainers are the way to go! For comfort and performance – there's no other trainer for **me!**"

Run faster, run harder, run better. It's a no-brainer: with **RunFaster** *trainers you can have it all.*

B.

Relax in Barbados...

Fed up with the damp British weather?

Fancy listening to the gentle lap of waves on a sandy beach?

Like the thought of sun-soaked, lazy afternoons by a pool?

Then look no further. Barbados Beach Breaks is the answer to your dreams.

• **Direct flights** • **Short transfer distance** • **Airport pick-ups** • **All-inclusive**

Delicious Caribbean food, sun, sand and sea – what more could you ask for?

From humble villages nestled in the hinterland to the nightlife of Bridgetown and Speightstown; relax on comfortable beach beds in the shade of a palm or experience water skiing in the bay; choose from light salads and snacks to six-course gourmet meals: you can have it all in sunny Barbados!

SPECIAL DEALS ON CATAMARAN CRUISES AND DAY TRIPS TO BRIDGETOWN IF YOU BOOK BEFORE MARCH!

1 Look at advert **A**.

a. What are the **two** main selling points of RunFaster trainers? **Tick two.** **(2 marks)**

style ☐   performance ☐

value for money ☐   comfort ☐

b. Why is Harry Hurdle's quote used in the advert? **(1 mark)**

....

c. What should you be able to do if you wear RunFaster trainers? **(1 mark)**

....

2 Look at advert **B**.

a. What does the company **Barbados Beach Breaks** offer that would make a holiday to Barbados easier for the customer? **(2 marks)**

....

....

b. Explain how the company makes sure there is something for everyone on Barbados. **(3 marks)**

....

....

....

3 Look at adverts **A** and **B**.
Tick the advertising features that each advert has used. **(3 marks)**

	A	B
Rhetorical questions		
Special offer		
Celebrity endorsement		

Total 12 —

Read this persuasive letter and answer the questions on the next page.

Dear Ms Christensen,

I am writing in response to your notice in last week's local paper that planning permission has been granted for the construction of a leisure centre in the woodland on the outskirts of town. I would like to persuade you to move the centre to the other side of the motorway.

Our woodland is a precious part of the community, used regularly by old and young alike. Eighty-five percent of people asked in a recent survey (conducted at my Save the Woodland coffee morning) confirm this. Can you really justify destroying this beloved area of natural beauty? It's shocking to think you would even consider such sabotage!

Other casualties would be our wildlife – did you know there are badgers, newts and rare frogs living in the woodland? Not to mention the birds. Where do you propose to relocate them? Bluebells are becoming rarer and rarer in the British Isles but we have been lucky enough to keep our blue spring blanket! And what a joy it is for us all!

Finally, a leisure centre (as our neighbouring town of Wilmshigh knows to their peril) attracts a lot of unpleasant characters, namely teenagers, who like to 'hang about' in the evenings making some of us feel quite uncomfortable going about our everyday lives. These youths smoke and swear and leave mountains of litter before they slouch off to wherever they live. Have you considered the extra cost to the council in tidying up their mess?

I do hope you will take my concerns very seriously. I am not normally one for complaining (that last letter about my neighbour's cat meowing too loudly was fully supported by other people on my street but thankfully has been resolved since the owners moved away). I very much look forward to your reply at your earliest convenience, but preferably before the end of this week, otherwise my Save the Woodland support team will be forced to spend the weekend making banners and posters for an early Monday morning protest march.

Yours sincerely,
Mrs Rothwell

1 What are the three main objections that Mrs Rothwell makes to the construction of a leisure centre on the woodland area?

a. .... **(1 mark)**

b. .... **(1 mark)**

c. .... **(1 mark)**

2 What metaphor does the writer use to describe bluebells in paragraph three? **(1 mark)**

....

....

3 Why might the results of Mrs Rothwell's survey be biased? **(1 mark)**

....

....

....

4 What is Mrs Rothwell's opinion of teenagers? Use evidence from the text to support your answer. **(3 marks)**

....

....

....

....

5 Explain why it is amusing when Mrs Rothwell states that she is 'not normally one for complaining'. **(2 marks)**

....

....

6 What mild threat does Mrs Rothwell make towards Ms Christensen? **(2 marks)**

....

....

Total ——
12

Read the newspaper article below and answer the questions on the next page.

TIGER ON THE LOOSE!

A TIGER was spotted yesterday near the Disneyland Paris theme park, triggering a large scale panic, with warnings for children to be picked up from school in cars and local residents to stay indoors.

Reports came in of sightings in two separate locations by two different people near the town of Montevrain, east of Paris, prompting a helicopter to be dispatched. Some 60 police and firemen, armed with stun guns, were scrambled to the edges of town to set up a security perimeter.

In the first sighting, a woman saw the beast prowling in a Montevrain supermarket car park. "I couldn't believe my eyes at first," said Marie-Claire Duval. "It came from nowhere and was simply huge. I bundled my petrified children into the car and rang the police." By the time officers arrived at the scene, the animal had gone.

The next report came from a man walking his dog in the local park, which caused police to widen the net of their search. However, even scouring every inch of the park was to no avail.

Officers were posted outside the town's schools to protect the children inside. "We've asked parents to come and fetch their children from school in cars so that no child goes home alone or without supervision," said Cedric Tartaud-Gineste, the mayor's chief of staff.

After almost 12 hours of hunting, the search proved fruitless. Feline experts analysed a paw print found in the park and surmised that it was most likely a tiger, with a weight of around 80 kg.

One spokesman from the zoo at a nearby town said the animal was quite likely a pet that had broken free of its enclosure; certainly there have been no reports of any escapes from either zoos or circuses.

Latest reports reveal that a deployment of French soldiers from a nearby army base was sent to join the hunt. Authorities are advising people to stay indoors until the beast has been caught.

If you have any information that might help the authorities with the search for this potentially dangerous animal, please contact info@tigerhunt.montevrain.fr

1 What is the meaning of the word 'triggering' in the first paragraph? **(1 mark)**

....

2 What two warnings were given after the report of the tiger sighting? **(2 marks)**

....

....

3 Explain what is meant by a 'security perimeter'. **(1 mark)**

....

....

4 What was Marie-Claire Duval's first instinct upon seeing the huge cat? **(1 mark)**

....

5 What phrase in paragraph four tells you that the police made a very thorough search of the local park? **(1 mark)**

....

6 'The search proved fruitless'. This means that: **(1 mark)**
Tick one.

a. The officers couldn't find any fruit. ☐

b. The search came to nothing. ☐

c. The officers were fed up after 12 hours. ☐

d. The search uncovered many clues. ☐

7 Where had the cat most likely come from? **(1 mark)**

....

Total —— 8

Fiction Writing

① Consider the following storyline:

A climber has fallen over a cliff edge, attached to his partner by a rope. He doesn't know if his partner, Tom, is going to be able to pull him up to safety as he can't communicate with him due to the howling wind.

The story has been started below.

Clinging desperately to the frozen rope, I focused on being positive; yet the longer I dangled there, limp and helpless, the more certain it seemed that I would meet my end. The icy wind cut into my face, my lips were numb, my eyelashes thick with frost. What was Tom doing up there? Suddenly the rope vibrated, then snaked violently, causing me to glance in horror at the bottomless pit of ice yawning below.

Now continue the story, using multi-sensory description and a range of figurative language, so that the reader can visualise the setting and empathise with the climber's fears as he tries to solve his dilemma. Plan your story before you start to write, using the planning boxes opposite.

When you have finished writing your story, self-edit and decide on a suitable title.

You should consider the following criteria when writing:
- enjoyment and engagement for the reader
- appropriate features for this genre
- interesting language and vocabulary choices
- variety of sentence starters, lengths and types
- a range of accurate punctuation.

Vocabulary bank

frost-bitten   shards of ice   in sheer desperation
inch by inch   treacherous

Top tip!

Stories with a back-drop of extreme weather provide great opportunities to use metaphors and personification, e.g. '… bottomless pit of ice yawning below.'

Planning

What next?

How the dilemma is solved

Ending

Title: ....

....

....

....

....

....

....

....

Continue your answer on a separate sheet of paper if you need to.

1 Consider the following storyline:

As a boy and his father are driving in their car, they enter a tunnel. However, this is no ordinary tunnel as they both soon find out…

The story has been started below.

Dad drove the car into the tunnel. Strange, I thought, that there weren't the usual lights overhead. Dad flicked the full beam on; we were the only vehicle in there. Staring out of the window, I noticed the tunnel walls were glistening with green slime. Despite the heater being on full-blast, the car felt suddenly chilly. The pin-prick of light in the distance told me we would soon be out but I still felt uneasy. I gulped and looked at dad; his knuckles were white as he gripped the steering wheel tightly. Something wasn't quite right… and when we finally emerged from the far end and looked around, we knew what it was…

Continue the story, keeping to the same genre (mystery, adventure, sci-fi – it could be a bit of all three!) and use appropriate language and punctuation to show tension and suspense. Decide on a suitable title when you have finished your story.

You should consider the following criteria when writing:
- enjoyment and engagement for the reader
- appropriate features for this genre
- interesting language and vocabulary choices
- variety of sentence starters, lengths and types
- a range of accurate punctuation.

Vocabulary bank

nail-biting   spine-chilling   in fear of our lives   gripped with fear

Self-edit by reading back over your writing to make it even better. Proofread for spelling, grammar and punctuation errors.

Top tip!

Planning

Ending

....
....
....
....
....
....

What next?

....
....
....
....
....

NARRATIVE

How the dilemma is solved

....
....
....
....
....

Title: ....

....

....

....

Continue your answer on a separate sheet of paper.

1 Read this concrete poem.

Star!
Shining bright
in the black velvet night.
A jewelled and twinkling comfort light.
A high golden diamond
Shining bright.
Star!

Now write your own concrete poem about the moon and the sun, using the shapes provided below. **(4 marks)**

2 Read this haiku.

> Springing to new life
> Flowers dance in the cool breeze
> Searching for warm sun.

Now try writing **two** haikus of your own, remembering to use five syllables on the first line, seven on the second and five on the third.

You could write about a season, the weather or any other aspect of nature.

(4 marks per haiku)

Haiku 1: ....

....

....

Haiku 2: ....

....

....

3 Read the first verse of this poem (called *Wonderful Mum*) which uses kennings, then add your own verse.

(4 marks)

She's a:
Sadness Soother
Meal maker
Reassuring cuddler
Story-teller
Personal protector
Sweetie supplier!

She's a:

....

....

....

....

Total —— 16

1 Write an information text about your school.

As you need to 'promote' your school so that other parents will want to send their children there, make sure you show it in a positive light. It does not necessarily have to be a true reflection of your own school.

You might want to use the planning grid on the opposite page to help you plan.

You should consider the following criteria when writing:

- enjoyment and engagement for the reader
- appropriate features for the genre
- interesting language and vocabulary choices
- variety of sentence starters, lengths and types
- a range of accurate punctuation.

Top tip! Remember to use subheadings to help you organise your text into sections.

Planning

Introduction
General information such as:
Where is your school?
How many pupils?
Name of Head Teacher

Sport
What sports / teams?
What competitions?

Music and Drama
What instruments / tuition does your school offer?
What performances?

School dinners
Healthy eating options?
Themed days, e.g. Chinese New Year?

Residentials
Where?
Who goes?

After-school clubs
What clubs?

Christmas and summer fair
Pupil involvement

....

....

....

....

....

....

Continue your answer on a separate sheet of paper if you need to.

Non-fiction Writing

❶ Write an explanation text titled 'How are seeds spread?' Explain how plant seeds are spread, using the Internet or a book to help you, plus your own knowledge from science lessons.

Use the suggested subheadings on the opposite page to help you plan. You can include pictures if you like but remember the writing is the most important element of your text!

You should consider the following criteria when writing:
- enjoyment and engagement for the reader
- appropriate features for the genre
- interesting language and vocabulary choices
- variety of sentence starters, lengths and types
- a range of accurate punctuation.

Vocabulary bank

dispersal   digestion   animal droppings   fruit   parent plant

Top tip!

Don't copy whole sentences directly from a book or website – this is called plagiarism. You must change the words into your own. This also shows that you have understood what you have read.

Planning

Tell the reader what you are going to be writing about in your introduction and say 'why' plants need to spread their seeds.

How animals spread plant seeds

How wind spreads plant seeds

How humans spread plant seeds

....

....

....

....

....

Continue your answer on a separate sheet of paper if you need to.

1 Create an advert for a 'healthy' burger that your company has produced, aimed at schools across the country.

You need to show that the ingredients satisfy the healthy eating policy in schools.

Remember to give your product a name and to use all the features of adverts to 'hook' or persuade the school to buy your product.

Write your advert on a separate piece of paper.

You should consider the following criteria when writing:
- enjoyment and engagement for the reader
- appropriate features for the genre
- interesting language and vocabulary choices
- variety of sentence starters, lengths and types
- a range of accurate punctuation.

2 Now write a persuasive letter to the Head Teacher of a local primary school to convince her/him that she/he should include your healthy burgers on their school dinner menu.

Remember to put your address on the top right-hand lines followed by the date, and the name and address of the Head Teacher on the left-hand side.

You should consider the following criteria when writing:
- enjoyment and engagement for the reader
- appropriate features for the genre
- interesting language and vocabulary choices
- variety of sentence starters, lengths and types
- a range of accurate punctuation.

Top tip! Remember: If you know the name of the recipient of your letter, you sign off 'Yours sincerely'.

Planning

Introduction – say why you are writing.

Give two or three reasons why the Head Teacher should buy your product.

Reason 1	Reason 2	Reason 3

_____

_____

_____

_____

_____

_____

_____

_____

_____

_____

_____

_____

_____

_____

Continue your answer on a separate sheet of paper if you need to.

1 Consider the information below.

Tom and his brother Sam visited London with their parents. Sam really enjoyed seeing all the sights, museums and art galleries, while Tom was bored stiff throughout the whole trip!

Write a short recount (chronological report) **from each boy's point of view**, starting with them getting on the train in the morning and ending with the return trip home that evening, saying what they did but also their opinions of the trip.

You could talk about a museum or art gallery visit, where you went for lunch and the transport you used to get around the city. **Write in the first person!**

Here are some ideas to help you:
* The Tower of London
* Buckingham Palace
* Thames river trip
* Westminster Abbey
* The Natural History Museum
* The Shard
* London Underground/the Tube

You should consider the following criteria when writing:
* enjoyment and engagement for the reader
* appropriate features for the genre
* interesting language and vocabulary choices
* variety of sentence starters, lengths and types
* a range of accurate punctuation.

Vocabulary bank

Before I knew it…	Packed like sardines
Once we were inside, we…	Despite the weather…
…thoroughly enjoyable… (Sam)	value for money (Sam)
…completely miserable… (Tom)	waste of money (Tom)

Planning

Places you visited in chronological order (remember to include lunch!) and what they were like/your personal opinion as **a)** Tom **b)** Sam.

Tom	Sam
•	• ....
•	• ....
•	• ....
•	• ....

Tom:

....

....

....

....

....

....

....

Sam:

....

....

....

....

....

....

....

Continue your answer on a separate sheet of paper if you need to.

1 There has been a sighting of a baboon-like creature on a local primary school playing field.

As a journalist, you have been sent to investigate before writing up your report for the evening edition of the local paper you work for.

The police and fire service are at the school when you get there, as are the two witnesses who spotted the creature: the school caretaker, Mr Mills, and Billy Bradshaw, a Year 6 pupil.

Remember to use the features of newspaper articles:

- headline (no more than seven words; try to use catchy words, alliteration, puns)
- by-line (who the article is by)
- lead paragraph – tells the reader who, where, when, why and what
- main body – tells the reader the details of how/why the event happened
- pictures with captions
- sources and/or eye-witnesses with quotes.

You should consider the following criteria when writing:

- enjoyment and engagement for the reader
- appropriate features for the genre
- interesting language and vocabulary choices
- variety of sentence starters, lengths and types
- a range of accurate punctuation.

Top tip!

Quotes are direct speech so they need to be in inverted commas.

the DAILY NEWS
NORTHWEST EDITION

BLIZZARDS BLAST BRITAIN

Yesterday most parts of the country were blasted by gale force winds and blinding blizzards as temperatures plummeted to well below freezing.

Planning

Who?	What?
Where?	**When?**
Why?	**How?**

Continue your answer on a separate sheet of paper if you need to.

1 Your school has just held a competition called 'Guess Who's Got Talent?'

You have been asked to write an article for the school magazine or newspaper, reporting on the acts and audience reaction.

Choose no more than four acts to report on, giving reasons why, in your opinion, some acts were excellent, whilst others weren't…

You should consider the following criteria when writing:
- enjoyment and engagement for the reader
- appropriate features for the genre
- interesting language and vocabulary choices
- variety of sentence starters, lengths and types
- a range of accurate punctuation.

Top tip! Try to show your own personality in your report – unlike a newspaper article, you can give your opinion about the acts. You might want to use humour to describe how some acts didn't work as they were intended to.

Top tip! Remember to include a summary in your article. It might be one line or a short paragraph.

READING

Fiction and non-fiction texts
pages 4–5

1 Answers will vary. Award 3 marks for at least 6 genres across fiction and non-fiction.

   Fiction – horror, romance, mystery, comedy, adventure, science-fiction, fantasy
   Non-fiction – explanation, information, instruction, persuasive, autobiography, biography, recount
   (3 marks; award only 2 marks for 4–5; 1 mark for 2–3)

2 To give you a brief summary of the book or to tell you what it is about. **(1 mark)**

3 Information or explanation texts. **(1 mark)**

4 A Galactic Journey – Science-fiction
   Cargo Ships of the World – Information text
   The Adventures of My Big Red Spotted Pants! – Comedy
   Detective Doogle and the Mystery Mansion – Mystery **(4 marks)**

Imagery and figurative language
pages 6–9
Figurative language

1 **a.** onomatopoeia **b.** assonance
   c. simile **d.** personification
   e. metaphor **f.** alliteration **(6 marks)**

Similes

1 Answers will vary. Appropriate similes to describe each subject. **(4 marks)**

Metaphors

1 Our last day in Year 6 was a rollercoaster of emotions. ☑ **(1 mark)**

2 **a.** My heart was a carpenter's busy hammer. **(1 mark)**
   b. The snow on the hills was a white, fluffy blanket. **(1 mark)**
   c. My tears were rushing rivers flooding down my cheeks. **(1 mark)**
   d. My best friend Ajamil is a walking dictionary. **(1 mark)**

Personification

1 Soon the two friends entered a clearing where the gnarled and twisted fleshless fingers of hunched trees brushed the forest floor in the wind. They couldn't afford to be afraid and there appeared to be a cave further along where they might take refuge. A sudden gust of wind attacked them from behind so they didn't stop to reconsider. Cautiously, the children entered the yawning cave which soon consumed them… **(4 marks)**

2 Accept appropriate answers where the mountain is given 'human qualities'. For example: The mountain was a sleeping giant lying on his back. **(2 marks)**

Onomatopoeia

1 **a.** The horse's hooves <u>clattered</u> across the cobbles. **(1 mark)**
   b. The bees were <u>buzzing</u> around the flowers. **(1 mark)**
   c. <u>Click</u>! Dad switched the fairy lights on. **(1 mark)**
   d. The drink <u>fizzed</u> over the top of my glass. **(1 mark)**
   e. The rain <u>bubbled</u> in the gutters. **(1 mark)**
   f. We could hear the leaves <u>rustling</u> in the wind. **(1 mark)**

2 Answers will vary. Examples:
   a. water: **splash** **(1 mark)**
   b. wind: **whoosh** **(1 mark)**
   c. cow: **moo** **(1 mark)**
   d. cat: **purr** **(1 mark)**
   e. horn: **beep** **(1 mark)**
   f. clock: **tick-tock** **(1 mark)**

Alliteration

1 **a.** The turtles slithered across the soft sand towards the sea. **(1 mark)**
   b. I dangled dangerously from the death-defying cliff edge. **(1 mark)**
   c. He held the bloodied blade above the beast's bedraggled body. **(1 mark)**
   d. Katie cooked cupcakes in her cosy kitchen. **(1 mark)**

2 Answers will vary. Examples (which show more than one example):
   a. lion   The lazy lion lounged in its lair. **(1 mark)**
   b. granny   My grumpy granny grumbled about the gravy. **(1 mark)**
   c. prince   Peter the perfect prince posted his parcel. **(1 mark)**
   d. wind   The wild wind whistled from the west. **(1 mark)**

Assonance

1 Creeping three at a time
   The creatures seek shelter
   From the whistling wind.
   Under the bright night sky,
   They hide inside and cry,
   Praying for day.
   (2 marks for assonance identified in 5–6 lines; 1 mark for 3–4 lines)

Fiction – narrative comprehension
pages 10–11
1. Kamuzu's brother ☑ **(1 mark)**
2. Longing for **(1 mark)**
3. That the baboons were raiding / eating the maize. **(1 mark)**
4. To try to scare the baboons away. **(1 mark)**
5. 'scavengers' **(1 mark)**
6. The maize was high and dense. **(1 mark)**
7. It helped Kamuzu orientate himself because he couldn't actually see anything. **(1 mark)**
8. *There*. is written in italics for dramatic effect. It is on its own line which further makes it stand out. It's almost like this is what Kamuzu says as he parts the maize stalks to find the baboons eating the maize. **(2 marks)**
9. The biggest, strongest or most important baboon of the group. **(1 mark)**
10. Normally he would have expected the baboon to run but it did the last thing he expected. **(1 mark)**

Fiction – poetry comprehension
pages 12–13
1. It's so stormy that the house is like a ship out at sea, tossed about on the waves. **(2 marks)**
2.

Text	What the author is comparing
The tent of **the hills** drummed and strained its guyrope	The hills are being compared to tents 'vibrating' due to the strong wind, with their guyropes pulled tight.
The house Rang like some fine green goblet	The house is being compared to a fragile glass; the ringing is the whistling of the wind.
We … feel the roots of **the house** move	The house is being compared to a plant – the roots are the foundations of the house that they feel move.

(3 marks)

3. The narrator is struggling to read, think or communicate with the other person in the house. **(1 mark)**
4. The wind is so strong that it appears to bend the gull like an iron bar. You would think that an iron bar would be impossible to bend so this demonstrates just how strong the wind is. **(2 marks)**
5. Answers will vary.
   Example: Hearing the stones cry out under the horizons.
   Why I think it is effective: This shows us that even the stones, which are hard and unbreakable, are in fear of the fierce weather – they 'cry out' like humans would do. **(1 mark)**

Fiction – poetry comprehension
pages 14–15
1. A bed is a soft and safe place but this one was not soft or safe for his son. **(2 marks)**
2. His son had been stung after falling in the nettles. **(1 mark)**
3. 'beaded' tells you the boy's skin had blistered and the bumps looked like beads. **(1 mark)**
4. The poet's son gave a weak smile; his heart wasn't in it. **(1 mark)**
5. He was sharpening the blade of his billhook. **(1 mark)**
6. He sharpened his billhook as if using it as a weapon and going to war, then 'slashed in fury with it'. Then he lit a fire to burn 'the fallen dead' which is a dramatic way of describing the nettles. **(2 marks)**
7. He says that due to the sun and the rain, 'tall recruits' had appeared behind the shed and his son would be stung again. **(1 mark)**

Non-fiction – information and explanation texts
pages 16–17
1. A difficult or unwelcoming place to live. **(1 mark)**
2. In the Arctic Ocean. **(1 mark)**
3. A large proportion of the ocean is frozen all year round. **(1 mark)**
4. The floating and moving ice. **(1 mark)**
5.

	The Arctic	The Antarctic
Sun does not rise in winter	✓	✓
Sun is low in the sky in summer	✓	✓
Most of the continent is high above sea level		✓
Scientists carry out research there		✓

(4 marks)

6. The continent is high above sea level and covered in thousands of metres of ice. **(2 marks)**

Non-fiction – information and explanation texts
pages 18–19
1. plants ☑ **(1 mark)**
2. It means the camel has its own water supply in its hump. **(1 mark)**
3. sustains **(1 mark)**
4. To keep as much fluid in their bodies as possible. **(1 mark)**
5. a. So they can grasp plants that they eat without losing moisture from their tongues. **(1 mark)**
   b. To protect them against spiky plants. **(1 mark)**

6 They have three stomachs, which re-digest
their food many times. **(1 mark)**

7 Camel dung. **(1 mark)**

Non-fiction – persuasive writing
pages 20–21

1 **a.** performance ☑
comfort ☑ **(2 marks)**

b. People often want to buy the product even
more if a celebrity promotes it. **(1 mark)**

c. Run faster, run harder and run better.
Also accept: You can have it all. **(1 mark)**

2 **a.** Any two of the following: direct flights;
airport pick-ups; short transfer distance;
all-inclusive. **(2 marks)**

b. Any three of the following: Some people might like
to visit the small villages in the hills, lie on beach
beds in the shade and eat light snacks while
others might prefer the nightlife in the towns,
water skiing and six-course gourmet meals.
(3 marks)

3

	A	B
Rhetorical questions	✓	✓
Special offer		✓
Celebrity endorsement	✓	

(3 marks)

Non-fiction – persuasive writing
pages 22–23

1 **a.** It is a precious part of the community. **(1 mark)**
b. Wildlife would be affected. **(1 mark)**
c. It would attract unpleasant characters. **(1 mark)**

2 'blue spring blanket'. **(1 mark)**

3 Mrs Rothwell conducted the survey at her
Save the Woodland coffee morning so all the
people present would have been in agreement
with her. **(1 mark)**

4 Mrs Rothwell doesn't like teenagers. She generalises
by saying 'they smoke and swear and leave
mountains of litter'. She uses words like 'slouch' and
'hang about' and she says they make some people
feel very uncomfortable. **(3 marks)**

5 Mrs Rothwell states that she is 'not normally one for
complaining' but then goes straight on to talk about
another letter of complaint she sent about a cat that
meowed too loudly. It is even funnier because she
says the owners moved house, which sounds as if
they wanted to get away from her. **(2 marks)**

6 If she doesn't hear from Mrs Christensen before
the end of the week, her support team would make
posters for a protest on Monday. **(2 marks)**

Non-fiction – newspaper articles
pages 24–25

1 'triggering' here means setting off or starting. **(1 mark)**

2 Children should be picked up from school in cars and
local residents were warned to stay indoors. **(2 marks)**

3 A 'security perimeter' means the police positioned
themselves around the outside of the town in order
to keep the residents safe and to look out for
the tiger. **(1 mark)**

4 Any one of the following: Not to believe what she saw;
to bundle her frightened children into the car. **(1 mark)**

5 'scouring every inch of the park'. **(1 mark)**

6 **b.** The search came to nothing. ☑ **(1 mark)**

7 An enclosure where it had been kept as a pet.
(1 mark)

FICTION WRITING

> Success Criteria grids have been provided for the
> questions on pages 27–29 and should be used for
> assessing your finished work. Make your decisions with
> support from an adult.
>
> • Tick **bronze** if you feel you are working towards that
>   element.
> • Tick **silver** if you feel you have achieved that
>   element.
> • Tick **gold** if you feel that you have excelled yourself
>   in that element.

Narrative
pages 26–27

1 Assess yourself using the success criteria grid. Accept
appropriate features used for descriptive narrative:
multi-sensory description and figurative language.

Success Criteria Grid	BRONZE	SILVER	GOLD
Enjoyment and engagement for the reader			
Appropriate features for the genre, e.g. figurative and descriptive language			
Interesting language and vocabulary choices			
Variety of sentence starters, lengths and types			
A range of accurate punctuation			

Narrative

pages 28–29

1 Assess yourself using the success criteria grid below.

Success Criteria Grid	BRONZE	SILVER	GOLD
Enjoyment and engagement for the reader			
Appropriate features for the genre, e.g. figurative and descriptive language			
Interesting language and vocabulary choices			
Variety of sentence starters, lengths and types			
A range of accurate punctuation			

Poetry

pages 30–31

1 Accept appropriate concrete poems. **(4 marks)**

2 Accept two haiku written according to their features. **(8 marks)**

3 Accept verse of kenning written according to its features. **(4 marks)**

NON-FICTION WRITING

Success Criteria grids have been provided for the questions on pages 32–45 and should be used for assessing your finished work. Make your decisions with support from an adult.

- Tick **bronze** if you feel you are working towards that element.
- Tick **silver** if you feel you have achieved that element.
- Tick **gold** if you feel that you have excelled yourself in that element.

Information texts

pages 32–33

1 Assess yourself using the success criteria grid.

Success Criteria Grid	BRONZE	SILVER	GOLD
Enjoyment and engagement for the reader			
Appropriate features for the genre, e.g. subheadings, bullet points			
Interesting language and vocabulary choices			
Variety of sentence starters, lengths and types			
A range of accurate punctuation			

Explanation texts

pages 34–35

1 Assess yourself using the success criteria grid.

Success Criteria Grid	BRONZE	SILVER	GOLD
Enjoyment and engagement for the reader			
Appropriate features for the genre, e.g. subheadings, bullet points			
Interesting language and vocabulary choices			
Variety of sentence starters, lengths and types			
A range of accurate punctuation			

Persuasive writing

pages 36–37

1 Assess yourself using the success criteria grid.

Success Criteria Grid	BRONZE	SILVER	GOLD
Enjoyment and engagement for the reader			
Appropriate features for the genre, e.g. bold product name, slogan, repetition, rhetorical questions, bullet points, special offer, etc.			
Interesting language and vocabulary choices			
Variety of sentence starters, lengths and types			
A range of accurate punctuation			

2 Assess yourself using the success criteria grid.

Success Criteria Grid	BRONZE	SILVER	GOLD
Enjoyment and engagement for the reader			
Appropriate features for the genre, e.g. rhetorical questions, emotive language, exaggeration, letter format, etc.			
Interesting language and vocabulary choices			
Variety of sentence starters, lengths and types			
A range of accurate punctuation			

Recount

pages 38–39

1 Assess yourself using the success criteria grid.

Success Criteria Grid	BRONZE	SILVER	GOLD
Enjoyment and engagement for the reader			
Appropriate features for the genre, e.g. events in chronological order			
Interesting language and vocabulary choices			
Variety of sentence starters, lengths and types			
A range of accurate punctuation			

Newspaper articles

pages 40–41

1 Assess yourself using the success criteria grid.

Success Criteria Grid	BRONZE	SILVER	GOLD
Enjoyment and engagement for the reader			
Appropriate features for the genre, e.g. headline, by-line, lead paragraph (who, when, what, where, why), main body containing sources, eye witnesses, quotes and picture with caption			
Interesting language and vocabulary choices			
Variety of sentence starters, lengths and types			
A range of accurate punctuation			

Newspaper articles

pages 42–43

1 Assess yourself using the success criteria grid.

Success Criteria Grid	BRONZE	SILVER	GOLD
Enjoyment and engagement for the reader			
Appropriate features for the genre, e.g. headline, introduction (telling reader who, when, what, where), three or four paragraphs covering acts performed and writer's opinion			
Interesting language and vocabulary choices			
Variety of sentence starters, lengths and types			
A range of accurate punctuation			

Informal speech

pages 44–45

1 Assess yourself using the success criteria grid.

Success Criteria Grid	BRONZE	SILVER	GOLD
Enjoyment and engagement for the reader			
Appropriate features for the genre, e.g. informal speech			
Interesting language and vocabulary choices			
Variety of sentence starters, lengths and types			
A range of accurate punctuation			

2 Assess yourself using the success criteria grid.

Success Criteria Grid	BRONZE	SILVER	GOLD
Enjoyment and engagement for the reader			
Appropriate features for the genre, e.g. informal speech			
Interesting language and vocabulary choices			
Variety of sentence starters, lengths and types			
A range of accurate punctuation			

GRAMMAR AND PUNCTUATION

Nouns and pronouns

pages 46–47

Nouns

1 a. We all ate the <u>pizza</u> and drank our <u>juice</u>. **(1 mark)**

   b. <u>Erin</u> swapped her <u>book</u> at the <u>library</u>. **(1 mark)**

   c. <u>Stella</u> dropped lots of <u>pencils</u> on the <u>floor</u>. **(1 mark)**

   d. The <u>girls</u> stopped talking and listened to their <u>teacher</u>. **(1 mark)**

   e. <u>Scarves</u>, <u>gloves</u> and <u>hats</u> – all were packed for the <u>trip</u>. **(1 mark)**

Expanded noun phrases

1 a. The beautiful blue butterfly landed on my bare shoulder. **(1 mark)**

   b. We had such a lot of courage in spite of the awful danger we were in. **(1 mark)**

   c. My old grandfather kept two herds of cows on his five-acre farm. **(1 mark)**

   d. Our local primary school has a well-stocked library full of interesting books. **(1 mark)**

   e. Sasha went to the beautiful islands of Guernsey and Jersey for his first ever holiday. **(1 mark)**

2 Answers will vary. Examples:

countryside	The never-ending countryside
determination	His relentless determination
disgust	My utter disgust
swarm	A dense swarm of bees

(4 marks)

Pronouns

1 a. Katie and <u>I</u> unwrapped the sandwich, then quickly ate <u>it</u>. **(1 mark)**

b. <u>They</u> brought Liam to see <u>us</u> last night. **(1 mark)**

c. After Miles had picked some flowers for <u>me</u>, <u>he</u> put <u>them</u> in the kitchen. **(1 mark)**

d. Sipping the smoothie slowly, <u>she</u> was sure <u>it</u> tasted rather odd. **(1 mark)**

2 a. The lady, **who** lived in the old cottage, moved to a new house. **(1 mark)**

b. The dog, **whose** owner was quite poorly, was very sad. **(1 mark)**

c. We had all eaten the vegetable pie, **which** tasted amazing! **(1 mark)**

d. There are lots of books **that / which** I still haven't read yet. **(1 mark)**

3 a. I've got all my books but I can't find yours. **(1 mark)**

b. Becca said the football was hers but Sam was sure it was his. **(1 mark)**

c. Mum said they were their towels but I knew they were ours. **(1 mark)**

d. I thought we were all going to my house but I'm happy to go to yours. **(1 mark)**

Adjectives and adverbs
pages 48–49

1 a. Freddy, that <u>naughty</u> boy in Year 2, was in <u>big</u> trouble yet again. **(1 mark)**

b. With his <u>new</u> football in his hands, Archie headed towards the <u>muddy</u> field. **(1 mark)**

c. Although Brogan was <u>nervous</u> about the test, he was nonetheless a <u>determined</u> boy. **(1 mark)**

d. Despite the <u>atrocious</u> weather conditions, the <u>well-known</u> team of explorers set off. **(1 mark)**

2 Answers will vary. **(4 marks: 1 mark for two appropriate adjectives in each sentence)**

Adjectives comparing two nouns

1 a. Matt is **older** than Thomas. **(1 mark)**

b. Freya's hair is **curlier** than her friend's. **(1 mark)**

c. I think the countryside is **more beautiful / less beautiful** than inner city areas. **(1 mark)**

d. Our homework was **more interesting / less interesting** this week than last week. **(1 mark)**

Adjectives comparing more than two nouns

1 a. Mia had the **longest** hair of all the girls in her class. **(1 mark)**

b. That actress had to be the **most fascinating / least fascinating** person I'd ever interviewed. **(1 mark)**

c. We had the **most intelligent / least intelligent** people on our quiz team. **(1 mark)**

d. It was the **most disgusting** meal we'd ever eaten. **(1 mark)**

Adverbs

1 Answers will vary but should be appropriate adverbs in context. Examples:

a. Far out to sea, the armada of ships moved **elegantly / swiftly** across the horizon. **(1 mark)**

b. Having just won the final, the team jumped **joyfully / enthusiastically** in the air. **(1 mark)**

c. We arrived **incredibly / unbelievably** early for the musical performance. **(1 mark)**

d. The children were all **desperately / incredibly** keen to finish their art. **(1 mark)**

Verbs and modal verbs
pages 50–51
Verbs

1 a. The fire <u>roared</u> in the dark night sky. **(1 mark)**

b. We <u>left</u> our towels on the beach. **(1 mark)**

c. The soldiers <u>fire</u> at the practice target. **(1 mark)**

d. The aim of the game <u>is</u> to <u>aim</u> high. **(1 mark)**

e. Somehow we always <u>manage</u> to <u>forget</u> someone! **(1 mark)**

f. When you <u>have finished</u>, <u>start</u> the next task. **(1 mark)**

2 a. <u>go</u>: present   <u>were</u>: past **(1 mark)**

b. <u>barks</u>: present   <u>are</u>: present **(1 mark)**

c. <u>see</u>: present   <u>was</u>: past **(1 mark)**

3 Since we moved house in September, I <u>have attended</u> a new school. **(1 mark)**

4 As we **were playing** with our new puppy, Mum **was hanging** out the washing. **(1 mark)**

Modal verbs to indicate degrees of possibility

1 a. We (may) be going away tomorrow but Dad (may) not be able to come. **(1 mark)**

b. Jon (may) play football this Saturday and if he does, he (could) be made team captain. **(1 mark)**

2 a. There (will) be heavy traffic, so Mum said we (must) leave early. **(1 mark)**

b. As Milo (can) speak French fluently, he (will) go to France on holiday this year. **(1 mark)**

Adverbs to indicate degrees of possibility

1 a. We <u>clearly</u> aren't going to get there on time in this heavy traffic. **(1 mark)**

b. It's <u>obviously</u> the rush hour since it's 5 o'clock. **(1 mark)**

c. Dad said that <u>perhaps</u> he would take us to the park later. **(1 mark)**

d. <u>Maybe</u> we should have taken the country roads. **(1 mark)**

2

Adverb	Certainty	Uncertainty
probably		✓
possibly		✓
definitely	✓	
clearly	✓	
perhaps		✓

(5 marks)

Prepositions and determiners
pages 52–53
Prepositions

1 a. Zac hid <u>behind</u> the settee while his sister Sophie sat <u>in</u> the chair. **(1 mark)**

b. Mum found James's socks <u>under</u> the bed <u>inside</u> his school shoes. **(1 mark)**

c. Monty the dog chased Tabitha the cat <u>round</u> the corner and <u>up</u> the tree. **(1 mark)**

d. We jumped quickly <u>off</u> the wall and hid <u>beneath</u> the oak tree. **(1 mark)**

e. We could make out a spider <u>on</u> the ceiling crawling <u>away</u> from its web. **(1 mark)**

2 Answers may vary.

a. My family and I are travelling **to / around** Cornwall **by** train. **(1 mark)**

b. High **above** the mountain, the sun shone fiercely. **(1 mark)**

c. Grace and Chloe lifted Benji **over** the garden gate. **(1 mark)**

d. I hope to visit Portugal again **before** next year. **(1 mark)**

3 a. similar **to** **(1 mark)**
b. according **to** **(1 mark)**
c. inspired **by** **(1 mark)**
d. equal **to** **(1 mark)**
e. complain **about / to** **(1 mark)**
f. interfere **with** **(1 mark)**
g. agree **with / to** **(1 mark)**
h. rely **on** **(1 mark)**
4 c. through / into ☑ **(1 mark)**

Determiners

1 a. <u>A</u> bird in <u>the</u> hand is worth two in <u>the</u> bush. **(1 mark)**
b. <u>The</u> early bird catches <u>the</u> worm. **(1 mark)**
c. <u>The</u> pen is mightier than <u>the</u> sword. **(1 mark)**
d. <u>An</u> apple each day keeps the doctor away. **(1 mark)**

2 a. We chatted for hours about **the** excellent trip. **(1 mark)**

b. After **a** stressful afternoon, we finally sorted it out. **(1 mark)**

c. Max put on **an** orange t-shirt before going out to play. **(1 mark)**

d. We had such **an** amazing time on holiday! **(1 mark)**

3. a. We had the time of <u>our</u> lives on <u>our</u> most recent holiday to Thailand. **(1 mark)**

b. <u>Her</u> pile of books fell off the table when she banged into it with <u>her</u> bag. **(1 mark)**

c. After a long time filling out <u>her</u> passport form, Mum stuck it in <u>its</u> envelope and posted it. **(1 mark)**

d. <u>Our</u> team celebrated <u>their</u> win by singing songs. **(1 mark)**

Conjunctions and subordinate clauses
pages 54–55
Conjunctions that join two clauses of equal importance

1 a. My mother likes to go to Spain on holiday <u>but</u> my father prefers France. **(1 mark)**

b. We couldn't make swimming tonight <u>for</u> our car wouldn't start. **(1 mark)**

c. I find long division really easy <u>yet</u> long multiplication really hard! **(1 mark)**

d. It was way past our bedtime <u>so</u> our parents chased us up to bed. **(1 mark)**

e. I would like some new sandals for the summer holidays <u>and</u> my sister needs a new swimsuit. **(1 mark)**

f. Mia hadn't a clue where the map was, <u>nor</u> did she really care. **(1 mark)**

2 Answers may vary.

a. Milo has a dog **but** he hasn't got a cat. **(1 mark)**

b. Seb likes carrots **and** he likes cabbage. **(1 mark)**

c. My sister is extremely tall **but / yet** I am exceptionally short. **(1 mark)**

d. The rain was very heavy **so** the children couldn't play football. **(1 mark)**

e. Douglas refuses to eat vegetables **nor** will he eat fruit. **(1 mark)**

Conjunctions that join a main clause to a subordinate clause

1 a. <u>Although</u> it was snowing very heavily, we still managed to make it to school. **(1 mark)**

b. We had a very enjoyable trip to the cinema <u>after</u> we'd eaten pizza and salad. **(1 mark)**

c. Sarah said we should meet at the shops <u>since</u> it was the easiest option. **(1 mark)**

d. <u>Whenever</u> my mum sees mud on the floor, she gets out the dustpan and brush. **(1 mark)**

2

Sentence	Main clause	Subordinate clause
Even though there was a poor turn-out, the performers had a great night.		✓
Once the children knew the method, **they could solve the word problems**.	✓	
We all rushed down to the shore, although it looked less inviting in the drizzle.	✓	
As the sun began to set, a few people ventured out into the cooler air.		✓

(4 marks)

3　c.　As Stella looked out across the sea to the distant horizon. ☑　**(1 mark)**

Sentence types
pages 56–57

1　Any two appropriate statements.　**(2 marks)**
2　Any two appropriate questions.　**(2 marks)**
3　Any two appropriate commands.　**(2 marks)**
4　Any two appropriate exclamations.　**(2 marks)**
5　Appropriate command verbs. Examples:
　a.　**Eat / finish** your breakfast immediately!　**(1 mark)**
　b.　**Stop / stand** at the pedestrian crossing and **look** both ways before you cross.　**(1 mark)**
　c.　**Finish / do** your homework then **give** it to your teacher.　**(1 mark)**
　d.　**Write / send** a thank-you note to your friends who bought you presents.　**(1 mark)**
6　Take the first road on the left, then turn left. – command
　How many more days until the holidays? – question
　What a wonderful surprise to see you! – exclamation
　It's a perfect day for a picnic. – statement
7　Appropriate questions for the answers. Examples:
　a.　How many children are there in your school?　**(1 mark)**
　b.　Where did you go on holiday last summer?　**(1 mark)**
　c.　What is your favourite food?　**(1 mark)**

Direct speech
pages 58–59

1　When Benji heard the thunder in the middle of the night, he said it was the loudest noise he'd ever heard. "Make it go away!" he shouted. His mum said that it couldn't hurt him and it might help to count the seconds between the thunder claps and the lightning bolts. "It's nature, sweetheart, and it won't last forever," she reassured him. "Come on, let's count together." "One, two, three, four…," they counted.

By eight, Benji was already asleep.　**(4 marks)**
2　a.　"I would really like to go to the cinema to see that new Spiderman film," Paul said**.**　**(1 mark)**
　b.　"We knew that eventually we would move to America," the children told their neighbours**.**　**(1 mark)**
　c.　"Start running now**!**" Jack screamed**.**　**(1 mark)**
　d.　Taylor said**,** "I hope I remembered to put the chocolate brownies in the basket**.**"　**(1 mark)**
　e.　"Have you brought your library book in today**?**" asked the librarian**.**　**(1 mark)**
3　Answers may vary, e.g.:
　a.　"Will you play football with me, Phillip?" asked Max.　**(1 mark)**
　b.　"Everyone can come to my house for tea!" announced Harry.　**(1 mark)**
　c.　"Score!" shouted the Year 6 spectators at the lacrosse team.　**(1 mark)**
　d.　"Could I have some extra time in the reading test?" Honor asked her teacher.　**(1 mark)**
4　Answers will vary. Examples:
　whispered; muttered; sighed; agreed; stuttered; uttered; shouted; roared; screamed; shrieked.
　(10 marks)

Active and passive voice
pages 60–61

1　Two appropriate sentences in the active voice.　**(2 marks)**
2　Two appropriate sentences in the passive voice.　**(2 marks)**
3　a.　The children were taken by their parents to the disco for the Year 6 treat.　**(1 mark)**
　b.　Everest was conquered by Sir Edmund Hillary and Sherpa Tenzing in 1953.
　　OR: Everest was conquered in 1953 by Sir Edmund Hillary and Sherpa Tenzing.　**(1 mark)**
　c.　The apple pie was burned by the cooks because the oven was too hot.　**(1 mark)**
　d.　The rubbish was thrown out by Millie when the bin started to overflow.
　　OR: When the bin started to overflow, the rubbish was thrown out by Millie.　**(1 mark)**
　e.　My big sister's tooth was extracted by the dentist.　**(1 mark)**
　f.　Finally, the Champion's Cup was won by the determined junior team.
　　OR: The Champion's Cup was finally won by the determined junior team.　**(1 mark)**
4　The angry wasps stung the children. – active voice
　My mother brought my friends and me to the cinema. – active voice
　A family was rescued from the blaze by a fireman. – passive voice

We were given an ultimatum by our teacher. –
passive voice

The thieves were being pursued by the police. –
passive voice

We left our picnic blanket by the edge of the river. –
active voice **(6 marks)**

5 Answers may vary.

  a. An enthusiastic dog-walker walked my energetic
dog all week.
OR: All week, an enthusiastic dog-walker
walked my energetic dog. **(1 mark)**

  b. The team completed the transatlantic race in
record time. **(1 mark)**

  c. The emergency team received three phone calls
last night.
OR: Last night, the emergency team received
three phone calls. **(1 mark)**

  d. The young journalist wrote a fascinating
newspaper article. **(1 mark)**

Parenthesis
pages 62–63

1 **a.** The children's books **(**all of which are a bit tatty
and worn**)** have finally been returned to the
school library. **(1 mark)**

  b. My brother Miles **(**the one who's mad about music**)**
is going to a concert tonight. **(1 mark)**

  c. How could anyone **(**even the most hard-hearted**)** not
look at that newborn puppy and smile? **(1 mark)**

  d. I've said it before **(**and no doubt I will say it many
times again**)** that I don't like being teased by
my big sister. **(1 mark)**

  e. Look in the far corner of the park **(**the spot
where there's a fountain**)** and you will see
the lads playing football. **(1 mark)**

  f. I'm very good at reading **(**and writing for that
matter**)** but I don't perform well in tests. **(1 mark)**

2 Answers will vary. Accept either brackets, dashes or
commas correctly placed.

  a. We went home (cold and wet) and had hot baths
and bowls of soup. **(1 mark)**

  b. With only minutes to spare – we had forgotten to
set our alarm clock – we managed to get the last
train. **(1 mark)**

  c. Imagine my delight when chicken and carrots, my
favourites, were served on the plane. **(1 mark)**

  d. The winning goal (scored by Rooney) was the best
of the match. **(1 mark)**

  e. My best friend's dad – Mr Weasley – took us to
school this morning. **(1 mark)**

  f. We went to the local cinema, the Odeon, to watch
the new Disney movie. **(1 mark)**

3 **d.** My brother, short but very strong, stopped the
thieves from getting away. ✓ **(1 mark)**

Apostrophes
pages 64–65

1 She's always late for school. **(1 mark)**

2 My mum's birthday is today. **(1 mark)**

3

Words in full	Contraction	Words in full	Contraction
We have	**We've**	They are	**They're**
There is	**There's**	I would	**I'd**
She is	**She's**	I am	**I'm**
Will not	**Won't**	Was not	**Wasn't**
They would	**They'd**	Should not	**Shouldn't**
Is not	**Isn't**	Shall not	**Shan't**

(6 marks)

4 **b.** We'll probably go to the caravan where there's
always so much to do. ✓ **(1 mark)**

5 **a.** My best friend's dog is really naughty. **(1 mark)**

  b. Mrs Smith's umbrella is broken. **(1 mark)**

  c. Sinead's homework was ruined by the rain. **(1 mark)**

  d. The sun's rays beat down on the arid
desert sand. **(1 mark)**

  e. That dog's barks could be heard for miles
and miles. **(1 mark)**

  f. The girls' books need to go back to the
library today. **(1 mark)**

  g. Our class's furniture is going to be replaced.
(1 mark)

6 **a.** It's almost dark so its best we head home
before it's too late to catch the bus. **(3 marks)**
✓ ✗ ✓

  b. Its been drizzling on and off all day
so it's time the weather made it's
mind up. **(3 marks)**
✗ ✓ ✗

SPELLING

Prefixes
pages 66–67

1 illogical, irrespective, disability, misapprehension,
implausible, inaccessible **(6 marks)**

2 **a.** disrespect **(1 mark)**

  b. misrepresent **(1 mark)**

  c. disagree **(1 mark)**

  d. misunderstanding **(1 mark)**

  e. misinterpreted **(1 mark)**

3 **b.** The teacher said my artwork was
incomplete. ✓ **(1 mark)**

  d. It is quite improbable that the stadium will
be finished by next year. ✓ **(1 mark)**

4 Answers may vary. Example:
Not functioning correctly. **(1 mark)**

Prefixes from Latin and Greek

1 a. two (1 mark)
   b. big OR over OR above (1 mark)
   c. distant (1 mark)
   d. half (1 mark)

2 Answers may vary. Examples:

auto		aqua	pre
autobiography	autograph	aquaplane	preview
automobile	automatic	aquarium	premeditated

(8 marks)

Suffixes

pages 68–69

1 A suffix is a letter or string of letters added to the end of a root word, changing or adding to its meaning. (1 mark)

2 a. dependable (1 mark)
   b. comfortable (1 mark)
   c. allowable (1 mark)
   d. replaceable (1 mark)
   e. reliable (1 mark)
   f. noticeable (1 mark)

3

	Adjective	Adverb
horror	horrible	horribly
terror	terrible	terribly
sense	sensible	sensibly
reverse	reversible	reversibly
audio	audible	audibly

(5 marks)

4 a. vicious (1 mark)
   b. malicious (1 mark)
   c. spacious (1 mark)
   d. gracious (1 mark)

5 a. We went on our Year 6 (residential) trip to the Lake District. (1 mark)
   b. After so many (financial) worries, the Head Teacher was relieved he could afford the PE equipment. (1 mark)
   c. Many people believed the teacher had been very (influential) in inspiring the children. (1 mark)
   d. The cheeky boy pulled different (facial) expressions as the teacher talked. (1 mark)

Suffixes from Greek

1 Answers will vary. Examples:

Suffix	Word	Meaning
phone	xylophone	A percussion instrument
meter	pedometer	A device which measures how far you walk.
logy	geology	The study of rocks
phobia	agoraphobia	A fear of public places

(8 marks)

Tricky spellings

pages 70–71

The rule "i before e except after c"

1 Answers will vary. Examples:
   field; piece; shield; ceiling; deceive; conceive (6 marks)

2 a. receipt (1 mark)
   b. deceive (1 mark)
   c. perceived (1 mark)
   d. ceiling (1 mark)
   e. conceived (1 mark)

3 a. foreign (1 mark)
   b. seize (1 mark)
   c. weird (1 mark)
   d. protein (1 mark)
   e. caffeine (1 mark)

Words ending in fer

1

Word	Add suffixes	Is the **fer** stressed?
refer	referral	✓
	reference	✗
	referred	✓
transfer	transferral	✓
	transference	✗
	transferred	✓
prefer	preference	✗
	preferred	✓

(10 marks)

Silent letters

1 A silent letter is a letter that we don't pronounce. (1 mark)

2 a. assign   b. debt   c. crumb
   d. nestle   e. condemn   f. honest
   g. foreign   h. sword   i. knowledge
   j. knot   k. scissors   l. receipt

(12 marks)

3 a. Wednesday   scissors   **(1 mark)**
  b. jostling   silhouette   **(1 mark)**
  c. receipt   succumbing   **(1 mark)**

Homophones
pages 72–73

1 A homophone is a word that sounds the same as another word but has a different spelling and different meaning. **(1 mark)**

2 d. I looked through the window and saw a huge bear ambling about in the garden. ☑ **(1 mark)**

3

Word	Homophone(s)	Word	Homophone(s)
pause	**paws**	whether	**weather**
piece	**peace**	find	**fined**
pour	**pore/poor/paw**	great	**grate**
knew	**new/gnu**	flower	**flour**
buy	**bye/by**	night	**knight**
sent	**scent/cent**	morning	**mourning**
profit	**prophet**	root	**route**

(14 marks)

4 a. We walked down the **main** road to get to the bus stop. **(1 mark)**
  b. **There** was a lot of traffic as it was rush hour. **(1 mark)**
  c. In addition, there was a hold up **due** to roadworks. **(1 mark)**
  d. We **guessed** that our bus would be very late. **(1 mark)**
  e. So we **proceeded** to walk to school instead. **(1 mark)**

Near homophones

1 Near homophones don't sound exactly the same but are similar enough for people often to misspell them. **(1 mark)**

2 a. The hot, sunny weather had a therapeutic (effect) on the whole family. **(1 mark)**
  b. The teacher gave the parents some great (advice) about the tests. **(1 mark)**
  c. The fireman couldn't gain (access) to the burning building. **(1 mark)**
  d. Last night the swimming pool was full of screaming (adolescents). **(1 mark)**
  e. I bought the latest (edition) of my favourite magazine. **(1 mark)**
  f. We all found it difficult to (accept) that our cat had gone. **(1 mark)**

SPEAKING AND LISTENING
Speaking to an audience
pages 74–75

A Success Criteria grid has been provided for the questions on pages 74–75 and should be used for assessing your finished piece of work. Make your decisions with support from an adult.

- Tick **bronze** if you feel you are working towards that element.
- Tick **silver** if you feel you have achieved that element.
- Tick **gold** if you feel that you have excelled yourself in that element.

1 Assess yourself using the success criteria grid. Accept appropriate features of a presentation; persuasive techniques, props, body language and expression to reinforce the point being made.

Success Criteria Grid	BRONZE	SILVER	GOLD
Enjoyment and engagement for the reader			
Appropriate features for the genre, e.g. persuasive techniques, expression, props and body language			
Interesting language and vocabulary choices			
Variety of sentence starters, lengths and types			
A range of accurate punctuation			

Interviewing
pages 76–77

1 Accept six open questions based on the information about Scott provided in the text. **(6 marks)**

SATs PRACTICE QUESTIONS
pages 78–82

Reading comprehension

1 a. The mushrooms. **(1 mark)**
  b. Our foot's in the door – personification
    heaving the needles – assonance
    So many of us! / So many of us! – repetition **(2 marks)**
  c. It tells us that the mushrooms grow closely packed together so that they are nudging each other. 'Shovers' implies that each one is fighting for its own space. **(2 marks)**
  d. It makes you visualise the mushrooms as furniture with their table leg stalks and flat shelf-like surface. **(1 mark)**

2 a. He heard that Robert Peary had just reached the North Pole so decided to head for the South Pole instead. **(1 mark)**

b. He didn't want anyone to tell Scott that he was trying to get to the South Pole. **(1 mark)**

c. He didn't want Scott to be aware that he was trying to get to the South Pole first. **(1 mark)**

d. It wasn't his original intention to go to the South Pole. He had been heading for the North Pole and only changed his mind when he heard that Peary had got there first. **(2 marks)**

Grammar, Punctuation and Spelling

1 <u>Cautiously</u>, the girls crept into the garden, treading carefully as they went. **(1 mark)**

2 When Sonia arrived at her dad's bedside, **Sonia**

she

could see that he had improved. There was a chair next to the bed and Sonia sat in **the chair**.

it

(1 mark)

3

Adjective	Noun
detailed	map
waterproof	rucksack

(1 mark)

4 <u>I've</u> – I have; <u>weather's</u> – weather is; <u>we've</u> – we have. **(1 mark)**

5 an exclamation **(1 mark)**

6 a. dashes/double dashes. **(1 mark)**

b. (a pair of) commas / (a pair of) brackets **(1 mark)**

7 a. We <u>love</u> to visit the seaside but last year it was a bit of a washout. **(1 mark)**

b. All through the school year we worked hard, but now <u>is</u> the time to relax. **(1 mark)**

8 Hassan played basketball **although** he had a sore wrist. **(1 mark)**

9 "Hurry up or you'll be late for school!" shouted my mum. "It's almost 9 o'clock." **(1 mark)**

10 "So you think you're going to win the match tomorrow, <u>do you?</u>" **(1 mark)**

11 a. Mum has been waiting for ages for Katie's bus but (it's) clearly late. **(1 mark)**

b. We're thrilled that (Jake's) birthday celebration wasn't ruined by the bad weather. **(1 mark)**

12 The family we met on holiday**,** all of whom were very pleasant**,** contacted us last week. **(1 mark)**

13 When I pack for a weekend away in the countryside, I take lots of warm clothes**:** sweaters, boots, gloves and a waterproof coat. **(1 mark)**

14 Now that we **have eaten** our breakfast, we can set off on our journey. **(1 mark)**

15 I will finish my homework project this evening. ✓ **(1 mark)**

16 My brother went to school today, <u>even though he wasn't feeling well</u>. **(1 mark)**

17 Mrs Courtney's antique vase suddenly tipped over.

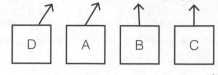

(1 mark)

18 accident ✓ **(1 mark)**

19 <u>Turn</u> to the next page and <u>read</u> the first two paragraphs. What do you think made Theo react that way? **(1 mark)**

Planning

Headline
Introduction

Who?   *What?*

Where?   *When?*

First paragraph (first act you will describe)

Second paragraph (second act you will describe)

Third paragraph (third act you will describe)

Fourth paragraph (fourth act you will describe)

Summary

....
....
....
....
....
....
....
....
....
....

Continue your answer on a separate sheet of paper if you need to.

1 Re-read the advert for Barbados Beach Breaks (on page 20). Imagine you are in Barbados, having a fabulous holiday! Write a postcard to your best friend, describing some of the activities you are doing and the people you have met. Remember to use informal speech.

John Jones

10, Oak Road

Derby

D1 2EM

2 Re-read the text about Kamuzu on page 10. Imagine you are Kamuzu, keeping watch, day after day, over village maize fields and protecting them from baboons.

Write two or three diary entries, ending up with the 'baboon raid'. Describe the heat, the boredom, the relentlessly long days. What would you rather be doing? Remember to use informal speech. The first entry has been done for you.

You should consider the following criteria when writing:
- enjoyment and engagement for the reader
- appropriate features for the genre
- interesting language and vocabulary choices
- variety of sentence starters, lengths and types
- a range of accurate punctuation.

Tuesday 3rd August

Another long day on my look-out post. Might as well not have bothered 'coz there weren't any baboons in sight. Bakili turned up half an hour late for his shift – what an idiot! He'd only been playing in the river with all his mates while I was burning up in the sweltering heat. I'll make him pay...

Wednesday 4th August

....

....

....

....

Thursday 5th August

....

....

....

....

....

Friday 6th August

....

....

....

....

....

Continue your answer on a separate sheet of paper if you need to.

Nouns

1 Underline all the **nouns** in these sentences.

a. We all ate the pizza and drank our juice. **(1 mark)**

b. Erin swapped her book at the library. **(1 mark)**

c. Stella dropped lots of pencils on the floor. **(1 mark)**

d. The girls stopped talking and listened to their teacher. **(1 mark)**

e. Scarves, gloves and hats – all were packed for the trip. **(1 mark)**

Expanded noun phrases

1 Circle all the expanded **noun phrases** in the following sentences.

a. The beautiful blue butterfly landed on my bare shoulder. **(1 mark)**

b. We had such a lot of courage in spite of the awful danger we were in. **(1 mark)**

c. My old grandfather kept two herds of cows on his five-acre farm. **(1 mark)**

d. Our local primary school has a well-stocked library full of interesting books. **(1 mark)**

e. Sasha went to the beautiful islands of Guernsey and Jersey for his first ever holiday. **(1 mark)**

2 Add suitable **determiners**, **possessive determiners** and **adjectives** to these nouns to create expanded noun phrases. The first one has been done for you. **(4 marks)**

puppy	*the mischievous little puppy*
countryside	....
determination	....
disgust	....
swarm	....

Pronouns

1 Underline the **pronouns** in the following sentences.

a. Katie and I unwrapped the sandwich, then quickly ate it.　　(1 mark)

b. They brought Liam to see us last night.　　(1 mark)

c. After Miles had picked some flowers for me, he put them in the kitchen.　　(1 mark)

d. Sipping the smoothie slowly, she was sure it tasted rather odd.　　(1 mark)

2 Complete these sentences with an appropriate **relative pronoun**.

a. The lady, ... lived in the old cottage, moved to a new house.　　(1 mark)

b. The dog, ... owner was quite poorly, was very sad.　　(1 mark)

c. We had all eaten the vegetable pie, ... tasted amazing!　　(1 mark)

d. There are lots of books .... I still haven't read yet.　　(1 mark)

3 Highlight the **possessive pronouns** in the following sentences.

a. I've got all my books but I can't find yours.　　(1 mark)

b. Becca said the football was hers but Sam was sure it was his.　　(1 mark)

c. Mum said they were their towels but I knew they were ours.　　(1 mark)

d. I thought we were all going to my house but I'm happy to go to yours.　　(1 mark)

Top tip! Relative pronouns introduce a relative clause and **refer back to** a noun.

Total ──
26

1 Underline **two adjectives** in each sentence.

a. Freddy, that naughty boy in Year 2, was in big trouble
yet again. **(1 mark)**

b. With his new football in his hands, Archie headed towards the
muddy field. **(1 mark)**

c. Although Brogan was nervous about the test, he was nonetheless a
determined boy. **(1 mark)**

d. Despite the atrocious weather conditions, the well-known team of
explorers set off. **(1 mark)**

2 Make these sentences more interesting by adding **adjectives** to
describe each noun.

a. The cat sat on the mat. **(1 mark)**

....

b. My sister came in and lay on the armchair. **(1 mark)**

....

c. My mum cooked our dinner. **(1 mark)**

....

d. We came across a field full of flowers. **(1 mark)**

....

Adjectives comparing two nouns

1 Turn the words in brackets into **adjectives that show a comparison**
between the two nouns in each sentence.

a. Matt is (old) .... than Thomas. **(1 mark)**

b. Freya's hair is (curly) .... than her friend's. **(1 mark)**

c. I think the countryside is (beautiful) ....
than inner city areas. **(1 mark)**

d. Our homework was (interesting) ....
this week than last week. **(1 mark)**

Adjectives comparing more than two nouns

1 Turn the words in brackets into suitable **adjectives that compare the subjects** with everyone or everything else in the sentences.

a. Mia had the (long) .... hair of all the girls in her class. **(1 mark)**

b. That actress had to be the (fascinating) .... person
I'd ever interviewed. **(1 mark)**

c. We had the (intelligent) .... people on our quiz team. **(1 mark)**

d. It was the (disgusting) .... meal we'd ever eaten. **(1 mark)**

Adverbs

1 Insert an appropriate adverb to say more about the **verbs** in these sentences.

a. Far out to sea, the armada of ships moved .... across
the horizon. **(1 mark)**

b. Having just won the final, the team jumped ....
in the air. **(1 mark)**

c. We arrived .... early for the musical performance. **(1 mark)**

d. The children were all .... keen to finish their art. **(1 mark)**

Use a thesaurus to find
more interesting adverbs to
use in your writing.

Top tip!

THESAURUS

DICTIONARY

Total $\frac{}{20}$

Verbs

❶ Underline the **verbs** in these sentences. There may be more than one in each.

a. The fire roared in the dark night sky.   **(1 mark)**

b. We left our towels on the beach.   **(1 mark)**

c. The soldiers fire at the practice target.   **(1 mark)**

d. The aim of the game is to aim high.   **(1 mark)**

e. Somehow we always manage to forget someone!   **(1 mark)**

f. When you have finished, start the next task.   **(1 mark)**

❷ Underline the **two** verbs in each of these sentences, then say whether they are **present** or **past** tense.

a. We regularly go to the cinema on Fridays but last week we were on holiday.   **(1 mark)**

   ....

b. Our dog barks at strangers but you are well-known to him. **(1 mark)**

   ....

c. I often see your brother at football training but he wasn't there yesterday.   **(1 mark)**

   ....

❸ Underline the verb that is in the **present perfect** in the sentence below.   **(1 mark)**

Since we moved house in September, I have attended a new school.

❹ Complete the sentence below using the **past progressive** form of the verbs in brackets.   **(1 mark)**

As we (play) .... with our new puppy, Mum

(hang) .... out the washing.

Modal verbs to indicate degrees of possibility

❶ Circle the **two modal verbs** indicating **possibility** in each of these sentences.

a. We may be going away tomorrow but Dad may not be able to come. **(1 mark)**

b. Jon may play football this Saturday and if he does, he could be made team captain. **(1 mark)**

❷ Circle the **two modal verbs** indicating **certainty** in each of these sentences.

a. There will be heavy traffic, so Mum said we must leave early. **(1 mark)**

b. As Milo can speak French fluently, he will go to France on holiday this year. **(1 mark)**

Adverbs to indicate degrees of possibility

❶ Underline the **adverb(s)** in each sentence that shows certainty or uncertainty.

a. We clearly aren't going to get there on time in this heavy traffic. **(1 mark)**

b. It's obviously the rush hour since it's 5 o'clock. **(1 mark)**

c. Dad said that perhaps he would take us to the park later. **(1 mark)**

d. Maybe we should have taken the country roads. **(1 mark)**

❷ Tick the correct box to indicate which adverbs in the paragraph below denote **uncertainty** or **certainty**. **(5 marks)**

> We probably won't be moving house before the summer. The builders might have difficulties finding the bricks we want and will possibly have to import them from abroad. It's definitely been a difficult time for Mum and Dad who clearly wanted us to be in well before the start of the school year.
> They've not had a minute to themselves and perhaps they will think twice about such a big project in the future.

Adverb	Certainty	Uncertainty
probably		
possibly		
definitely		
clearly		
perhaps		

Total ―― 24

Prepositions

1 Highlight the two **prepositions** that show **place** or **position** in each sentence.

a. Zac hid behind the settee while his sister Sophie sat in the chair.

(1 mark)

b. Mum found James's socks under the bed inside his school shoes.

(1 mark)

c. Monty the dog chased Tabitha the cat round the corner and up the tree.

(1 mark)

d. We jumped quickly off the wall and hid beneath the oak tree.

(1 mark)

e. We could make out a spider on the ceiling crawling away from its web.

(1 mark)

2 Complete the sentences with suitable **prepositions**.

a. My family and I are travelling .... Cornwall

.... train.

(1 mark)

b. High .... the mountain, the sun shone fiercely.

(1 mark)

c. Grace and Chloe lifted Benji .... the garden gate.

(1 mark)

d. I hope to visit Portugal again .... next year.

(1 mark)

3 Insert an appropriate preposition after each of the following words.

a. similar .... **(1 mark)**   **b.** according................... **(1 mark)**

c. inspired .... **(1 mark)**   **d.** equal .... **(1 mark)**

e. complain .... **(1 mark)**   **f.** interfere .... **(1 mark)**

g. agree .... **(1 mark)**   **h.** rely .... **(1 mark)**

4 Which pair of prepositions is most suitable for this sentence? **Tick one.**   **(1 mark)**

The thief escaped by climbing .... a window and .... a getaway car.

a. into/on ☐   b. onto/through ☐

c. through/into ☐   d. behind/onto ☐

Determiners

1 Underline all the **determiners** in these proverbs.

a. A bird in the hand is worth two in the bush.   **(1 mark)**

b. The early bird catches the worm.   **(1 mark)**

c. The pen is mightier than the sword.   **(1 mark)**

d. An apple each day keeps the doctor away.   **(1 mark)**

2 Insert an appropriate determiner in the following sentences where they are missing.

a. We chatted for hours about .... excellent trip.   **(1 mark)**

b. After .... stressful afternoon, we finally sorted it out.   **(1 mark)**

c. Max put on .... orange t-shirt before going out to play.   **(1 mark)**

d. We had such .... amazing time on holiday!   **(1 mark)**

3 Underline the two **possessives** acting as determiners in these sentences.

a. We had the time of our lives on our most recent holiday to Thailand.   **(1 mark)**

b. Her pile of books fell off the table when she banged into it with
her bag.   **(1 mark)**

c. After a long time filling out her passport form, Mum stuck it in its
envelope and posted it.   **(1 mark)**

d. Our team celebrated their win by singing songs.   **(1 mark)**

Top tip! Remember the determiner
an is always used before a
word starting with a vowel.

Total —
30

Conjunctions that join two clauses of equal importance

❶ Underline the **coordinating conjunctions** in the following sentences.

a. My mother likes to go to Spain on holiday but my father prefers France.

(1 mark)

b. We couldn't make swimming tonight for our car wouldn't start.

(1 mark)

c. I find long division really easy yet long multiplication really hard!

(1 mark)

d. It was way past our bedtime so our parents chased us up to bed.

(1 mark)

e. I would like some new sandals for the summer holidays and my sister needs a new swimsuit.

(1 mark)

f. Mia hadn't a clue where the map was, nor did she really care.

(1 mark)

❷ Link the sentences together with an appropriate coordinating conjunction. You might need to replace **nouns** with **pronouns**.

a. Milo has a dog. Milo hasn't got a cat. **(1 mark)**

b. Seb likes carrots. Seb likes cabbage. **(1 mark)**

c. My sister is extremely tall. I am exceptionally short. **(1 mark)**

d. The rain was very heavy. The children couldn't play football. **(1 mark)**

e. Douglas refuses to eat vegetables. Douglas will not eat fruit. **(1 mark)**

Remember: a conjunction can join two words, phrases or clauses.
apples **and** oranges
full of goodness **but** not fattening
I'd like to go home now, **although** I've really enjoyed my time here.

Conjunctions that join a main clause to a subordinate clause

1 Underline the **subordinating conjunctions** that link a **main clause** to a **subordinate clause** in the following sentences.

a. Although it was snowing very heavily, we still managed to make it to school.

(1 mark)

b. We had a very enjoyable trip to the cinema after we'd eaten pizza and salad.

(1 mark)

c. Sarah said we should meet at the shops since it was the easiest option. **(1 mark)**

d. Whenever my mum sees mud on the floor, she gets out the dustpan and brush.

(1 mark)

2 Tick the correct box to indicate whether the words in bold are **main clauses** or **subordinate clauses**.

(4 marks)

Sentence	Main clause	Subordinate clause
Even though there was a poor turn-out, the performers had a great night.		
Once the children knew the method, **they could solve the word problems**.		
We all rushed down to the shore, although it looked less inviting in the drizzle.		
As the sun began to set, a few people ventured out into the cooler air.		

3 Tick the sentence which is grammatically **incorrect**. **Tick one.**

(1 mark)

a. When she saw the size of the wolf, Erin screamed in terror.

b. There's no point having breakfast now because it's almost lunchtime.

c. As Stella looked out across the sea to the distant horizon.

d. In the middle of the night, as all went quiet, I heard a wolf howl.

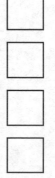

Total ——
20

① Write **two** examples of a **statement**.

a. .... **(1 mark)**

b. .... **(1 mark)**

② Write **two** examples of a **question**.

a. .... **(1 mark)**

b. .... **(1 mark)**

③ Write **two** examples of a **command**.

a. .... **(1 mark)**

b. .... **(1 mark)**

④ Write **two** examples of an **exclamation**.

a. .... **(1 mark)**

b. .... **(1 mark)**

⑤ Use **command verbs** to complete these sentences.

a. .... your breakfast immediately! **(1 mark)**

b. .... at the pedestrian crossing and

.... both ways before you cross. **(1 mark)**

c. .... your homework then ....
it to your teacher. **(1 mark)**

d. .... a thank-you note to
your friends who bought you presents. **(1 mark)**

6 Tick the correct box to indicate the sentence type.   **(4 marks)**

Sentence	Statement	Question	Command	Exclamation
Take the first road on the left, then turn left.				
How many more days until the holidays?				
What a wonderful surprise to see you!				
It's a perfect day for a picnic.				

7 Write questions to match these answers.

a. .... **(1 mark)**

There are approximately 250 children in my school.

b. .... **(1 mark)**

We went to Europe for two weeks and had a weekend in Scotland.

c. .... **(1 mark)**

Pizza, salad and coleslaw.

Top tip!

It makes sense that an exclamation mark comes at the end of an exclamation and a question mark at the end of a question! Often an exclamation mark comes at the end of a command too.

Total $\frac{}{19}$

1 Underline the **direct speech** in the following passage. **(4 marks)**

When Benji heard the thunder in the middle of the night, he said it was the loudest noise he'd ever heard.

"Make it go away!" he shouted. His mum said that it couldn't hurt him and it might help to count the seconds between the thunder claps and the lightning bolts.

"It's nature, sweetheart, and it won't last forever," she reassured him. "Come on, let's count together."

"One, two, three, four…," they counted. By eight, Benji was already asleep.

2 The following sentences are examples of direct speech but all the punctuation has been left out.
Rewrite, inserting **all** the missing punctuation in the correct places.
An example has been done for you.

We really should visit Grandma this afternoon said Mum

"We really should visit Grandma this afternoon," said Mum.

a. I would really like to go to the cinema to see that new Spiderman film Paul said **(1 mark)**

....

....

b. We knew that eventually we would move to America the children told their neighbours **(1 mark)**

....

....

c. Start running now Jack screamed **(1 mark)**

....

d. Taylor said I hope I remembered to put the chocolate brownies in the basket **(1 mark)**

....

e. Have you brought your library book in today asked the librarian **(1 mark)**

....

3 Rewrite these sentences using **inverted commas** to show what the person said (direct speech), changing any other punctuation as necessary.

a. Max asked Phillip if he would play football with him. **(1 mark)**

....

b. Harry announced that everyone could come to his house for tea. **(1 mark)**

....

c. All the Year 6 spectators shouted at the lacrosse team to score. **(1 mark)**

....

d. Honor asked her teacher if she could have some extra time in the reading test.

(1 mark)

....

4 How many words to replace **said** when using direct speech can you think of?

(10 marks)

....	....	....	....	....
....	....	....	....	....

Top tip!

Use a range of different words for **said** to make your writing more interesting.

Total $\frac{}{23}$

Active and passive voice

1 Write **two** sentences in the **active voice**.

a. .... (1 mark)

b. .... (1 mark)

2 Write **two** sentences in the **passive voice**.

a. .... (1 mark)

b. .... (1 mark)

3 Turn these sentences from the **active** to the **passive** voice.

a. The children's parents took them to the disco for the Year 6 treat.

(1 mark)

....

b. Sir Edmund Hillary and Sherpa Tenzing conquered Everest in 1953.

(1 mark)

....

c. The cooks burned the apple pie because the oven was too hot.

(1 mark)

....

d. When the bin started to overflow, Millie threw out the rubbish.

(1 mark)

....

e. The dentist extracted my big sister's tooth. **(1 mark)**

....

f. Finally, the determined junior team won the Champion's Cup.

(1 mark)

....

....

4 Tick the correct box to show whether the following sentences are in the **active voice** or the **passive voice**.

Sentence	Active voice	Passive voice
The angry wasps stung the children.		
My mother brought my friends and me to the cinema.		
A family was rescued from the blaze by a fireman.		
We were given an ultimatum by our teacher.		
The thieves were being pursued by the police.		
We left our picnic blanket by the edge of the river.		

(6 marks)

5 Turn these sentences from the **passive** voice into the **active** voice.

a. My energetic dog was walked all week by an enthusiastic dog-walker. **(1 mark)**

....

b. The transatlantic race was completed by the team in record time. **(1 mark)**

....

c. Three phone calls were received by the emergency team last night. **(1 mark)**

....

d. The newspaper article written by the young journalist was fascinating. **(1 mark)**

....

Total $\frac{}{20}$

1 Insert brackets to show **parenthesis** in each sentence.

a. The children's books all of which are a bit tatty and worn have finally been returned to the school library. **(1 mark)**

b. My brother Miles the one who's mad about music is going to a concert tonight. **(1 mark)**

c. How could anyone even the most hard-hearted not look at that newborn puppy and smile? **(1 mark)**

d. I've said it before and no doubt I will say it many times again that I don't like being teased by my big sister. **(1 mark)**

e. Look in the far corner of the park the spot where there's a fountain and you will see the lads playing football. **(1 mark)**

f. I'm very good at reading and writing for that matter but I don't perform well in tests. **(1 mark)**

Top tip! Information in parenthesis is often extra information and therefore less important than the information in the main clause.

2 Insert appropriate punctuation in each sentence so that the extra information is indicated by **parenthesis**.

a. We went home cold and wet and had hot baths and bowls of soup. **(1 mark)**

b. With only minutes to spare we had forgotten to set our alarm clock we managed to get the last train. **(1 mark)**

c. Imagine my delight when chicken and carrots my favourites were served on the plane. **(1 mark)**

d. The winning goal scored by Rooney was the best of the match. **(1 mark)**

e. My best friend's dad Mr Weasley took us to school this morning. **(1 mark)**

f. We went to the local cinema the Odeon to watch the new Disney movie. **(1 mark)**

③ Which sentence uses **commas** correctly to show parenthesis?
Tick one. **(1 mark)**

a. There was a lot, of fuss unnecessarily, after the ice-cream turned out to be the wrong flavour. ☐

b. Ruby not usually, a competitive girl, was first to fling herself over the finish line. ☐

c. When we reached the summit exhausted but exhilarated, we all cheered. ☐

d. My brother, short but very strong, stopped the thieves from getting away. ☐

Top tip!

The words in parenthesis are often relative clauses with the relative pronouns omitted. For example: My dinner, ready since 6 o'clock, was starting to turn cold. My dinner, which had been ready since 6 o'clock, was starting to turn cold.

Total —— 13

1 Insert the missing **apostrophe** to show a **contraction** in the sentence below.

Shes   always   late   for   school.   **(1 mark)**

2 Insert the missing apostrophe to show **possession** in the sentence below.

My   mums   birthday   is   today.   **(1 mark)**

3 **Contract** the following using an **apostrophe**.   **(6 marks)**

Words in full	Contraction	Words in full	Contraction
We have	....	They are	....
There is	....	I would	....
She is	....	I am	....
Will not	....	Was not	....
They would	....	Should not	....
Is not	....	Shall not	....

4 Which sentence uses **apostrophes for contraction** correctly?

(1 mark)

a. Iv'e not had my holiday yet because my dads' been too busy at work. ☐

b. We'll probably go to the caravan where there's always so much to do. ☐

c. My cousins' coming to join us for two days whichl'l be fun. ☐

d. Ther'es not much else Iw'd rather do. ☐

5 Change these sentences so that they contain **apostrophes to show possession**.

a. The dog belonging to my best friend is really naughty.   **(1 mark)**

....

b. The umbrella that belongs to Mrs Smith is broken.   **(1 mark)**

....

c. The homework belonging to Sinead was ruined by the rain. **(1 mark)**

....

d. The rays of the sun beat down on the arid desert sand. **(1 mark)**

....

e. The barks of that dog could be heard for miles and miles. **(1 mark)**

....

f. The books belonging to the girls need to go back to the library today. **(1 mark)**

....

g. The furniture belonging to our class is going to be replaced. **(1 mark)**

....

6 Decide whether the following have used **its** or **it's** correctly.
Put a tick ✓ or cross ✗ in the boxes.

a. It's almost dark so its best we head home before it's too late to catch the bus.

(3 marks)

b. Its been drizzling on and off all day so it's time the weather made it's mind up.

(3 marks)

Total ——
22

1 Match each **prefix** with a word to make a new word that is opposite in meaning. **(6 marks)**

Prefix	Word	New word
il	accessible	....
ir	ability	....
dis	apprehension	....
mis	logical	....
im	respective	....
in	plausible	....

2 Rewrite the words in brackets to give them a negative meaning by adding the prefixes **dis** or **mis**.

a. He showed (respect) .... by calling out while the teacher was speaking. **(1 mark)**

b. We don't want to (represent) .... the facts by exaggerating. **(1 mark)**

c. Please don't (agree) .... with me – you know I'm right! **(1 mark)**

d. The whole thing has been a total (understanding) .... **(1 mark)**

e. I think you have (interpreted) .... what I was trying to say. **(1 mark)**

3 Tick the **two** sentences that use **prefixes** correctly.
Tick two. **(2 marks)**

a. I think the football team were somewhat disguided by their coach. ☐

b. The teacher said my artwork was incomplete. ☐

c. Although the puppies are from the same litter, they are quite unsimilar. ☐

d. It is quite improbable that the stadium will be finished by next year. ☐

4 If you add the prefix **mal** to the word 'odorous', you make the word 'malodorous', meaning 'smells bad'. Add **mal** to the word 'practice' and you get 'malpractice', meaning 'bad practice'. Can you work out what **malfunction** means? **(1 mark)**

....

Prefixes from Latin and Greek

1 What do these **prefixes** mean?

a. bi   e.g. bilingual; bicycle   .... **(1 mark)**

b. super   e.g. supermarket; superhuman .... **(1 mark)**

c. tele   e.g. telescope; television   .... **(1 mark)**

d. semi   e.g. semi-circle; semi-detached .... **(1 mark)**

2 How many words can you think of that begin with the prefixes **auto**, **aqua** and **pre**? Write them below. **(8 marks)**

auto	
....	....
....	....
aqua	
....	....
pre	
....	....

Top tip!

Anything with **anti** as its prefix is going to have an opposite meaning to the original word. 'Anti-clockwise' means the opposite to 'clockwise'; 'anti-bullying' means being opposed to 'bullying'.

Total —
26

① What is a **suffix**? **(1 mark)**

....

② Add the suffix **able** to the following root words, remembering to apply any spelling rules.

   a. depend .... **(1 mark)**

   b. comfort .... **(1 mark)**

   c. allow .... **(1 mark)**

   d. replace .... **(1 mark)**

   e. rely .... **(1 mark)**

   f. notice .... **(1 mark)**

③ Add the suffixes **ible** and **ibly** to these words to make adjectives and adverbs. **(5 marks)**

	Adjective	**Adverb**
horror	....	....
terror	....	....
sense	....	....
reverse	....	....
audio	....	....

④ Add the suffix **cious** to these nouns, remembering to apply any spelling rules.

   a. vice .... **(1 mark)**

   b. malice .... **(1 mark)**

   c. space .... **(1 mark)**

   d. grace .... **(1 mark)**

5 Circle the word in bold that uses the correct suffix in the sentences below.

    a. We went on our Year 6 **residential/residencial** trip to the Lake District.   **(1 mark)**

    b. After so many **financial/finantial** worries, the Head Teacher was relieved he could afford the PE equipment.   **(1 mark)**

    c. Many people believed the teacher had been very **influential/influencial** in inspiring the children.   **(1 mark)**

    d. The cheeky boy pulled different **fatial/facial** expressions as the teacher talked.   **(1 mark)**

Suffixes from Greek

1 Write a word for each of the suffixes **phone**, **meter**, **logy** and **phobia**, then write its meaning.   **(8 marks)**

Suffix	Word(s)	Meaning
phone		
meter		
logy		
phobia		

Total $\dfrac{}{28}$

The rule 'i before e except after c but only when it rhymes with bee'

1 Write words that follow the 'i before e except after c <u>but only when it rhymes with bee</u>' rule. **(6 marks)**

....

....

....

2 Underline the correct spelling of the words in brackets in these sentences.

a. After searching high and low, I eventually found my (receipt / reciept). **(1 mark)**

b. I didn't want to (decieve / deceive) my mum so I told her about the torn book. **(1 mark)**

c. The teachers (percieved / perceived) that the child had been bullied. **(1 mark)**

d. My dad pulled a muscle in his back while painting the (cieling / ceiling). **(1 mark)**

e. The idea was (conceived / concieved) by the school council members. **(1 mark)**

3 The following anagrams make words that have an **ei** spelling, despite not coming after a soft **c**. Write the correctly spelled word next to the anagram.

a. rofgein .... **(1 mark)**

b. seezi .... **(1 mark)**

c. driew .... **(1 mark)**

d. tropien .... **(1 mark)**

e. finecafe .... **(1 mark)**

Words ending in fer

1 Add the suffixes **al**, **ence** and **ed** to the words on the left, then tick the correct box to indicate whether the **fer** sound is stressed or unstressed. **(10 marks)**

Word	Add suffixes	Is the **fer** stressed? ✓/✗
refer	**al**:	
	ence:	
	ed:	
transfer	**al**:	
	ence:	
	ed:	
prefer	**ence**:	
	ed:	

Silent letters

1 Explain what is meant by a **silent letter**. **(1 mark)**

....

2 Underline the silent letters in the following words. **(12 marks)**

a. assign   **b.** debt   **c.** crumb   **d.** nestle   **e.** condemn   **f.** honest

g. foreign   **h.** sword   **i.** knowledge   **j.** knot   **k.** scissors   **l.** receipt

3 The words in bold in the following sentences have had their silent letters removed. Rewrite the words using the correct spelling.

a. Last **Wenesday** I went to buy some **sissors** in town. **(1 mark)**

....

b. Despite the **josling** crowds, I finally found some writing paper with a **silouette** of a flower in the corner. **(1 mark)**

....

c. I put my **receit** safely in my bag and had a drink before **succuming** to the rush hour traffic. **(1 mark)**

....

Homophones

1 Write a definition for the word **homophone**.   **(1 mark)**

....

2 Each of the following sentences contains words in bold that are
homophones. Tick the **one** which has used the right ones.   **(1 mark)**

   a. We weren't **aloud** to **waist** food as mum was always very
      conscious of people who were starving.

   b. There was a **pear** of shoes on the **stares** that I had never
      seen before.

   c. I couldn't **bare** him when we were growing up but now
      we are **to** old to squabble.

   d. I looked **through** the window and saw a huge **bear**
      ambling about in the garden.

3 Match these words up with a homophone. For some, you may find
more than one.   **(14 marks)**

Word	Homophone(s)	Word	Homophone(s)
pause		whether	
piece		find	
pour		great	
knew		flower	
buy		night	
sent		morning	
profit		root	

4 Choose the correct word to complete each sentence below.   **(1 mark)**

   a. main / mane

      We walked down the .... road to get to
      the bus stop.

b. They're / There (1 mark)

.... was a lot of traffic as it was rush hour.

c. due / dew (1 mark)

In addition, there was a hold up .... to roadworks.

d. guest / guessed (1 mark)

We .... that our bus would be very late.

e. proceeded / preceded (1 mark)

So we .... to walk to school instead.

Near homophones

1 Explain what **near homophones** are. (1 mark)

....

2 Circle the correct word in the following sentences.

a. The hot, sunny weather had a therapeutic **effect/affect** on
the whole family. (1 mark)

b. The teacher gave the parents some great **advise/advice** about the tests. (1 mark)

c. The fireman couldn't gain **access/excess** to the burning building. (1 mark)

d. The swimming pool was full of screaming **adolescents/adolescence**. (1 mark)

e. I bought the latest **edition/addition** of my favourite magazine. (1 mark)

f. We all found it difficult to **accept/except** that our cat had gone. (1 mark)

> **Top tip!**
>
> To help you remember **practice/practise**:
> **practice** with a **c** is a **noun**; **c** comes
> before **n** in the alphabet; **practise** with an **s**
> is a **verb**; **s** comes before **v** in the alphabet.
>
> This also works with **advice/advise**!

Total 28

1 Write a presentation about one of the following subjects.

- The importance of a smart school uniform.
- Animals should not be kept in zoos.
- There's a time and a place for technology.
- Home is for home life, work is for school: schools should not hand out homework to primary school children.

Use props, body language and expression to support what you talk about.

Remember to use **persuasive techniques** to bring your audience round to your point of view.

Try to learn as much of it by heart as possible, then jot down key words and phrases on cards or Post-its before practising in front of a mirror and then in front of family or friends.

You might want to record your presentation so you can evaluate and improve it.

You should consider the following criteria when writing:
- enjoyment and engagement for the reader
- appropriate features for the genre
- interesting language and vocabulary choices
- variety of sentence starters, lengths and types
- a range of accurate punctuation.

Top tip!

Use hand and arm movements to emphasise points you feel emotional about. Perhaps bang your fist on the table to really drive a point home!

Planning

1. Introduction – tell your audience what you are going to be speaking about.

2. Three or four main points with supporting evidence.

3. Summary

....

....

....

....

....

....

....

Continue your answer on a separate sheet of paper if you need to.

1 Read the text below about the explorer Robert Falcon Scott.

Scott of the Antarctic. Who was he?

Scott of the Antarctic is a nickname that has been given to the famous British naval officer and explorer Robert Falcon Scott. From a very early age, however, he was known as 'Con' (from the name Falcon). Con joined the navy at the age of 13 and rose through the ranks over the next few years of his life. In late 1911 he led an expedition into unknown areas of Antarctica, aiming to become the first man to stand at the South Pole. On 17 January 1912, Scott reached his destination.

It's cold there. So what do you wear?

Modern polar explorers wear several layers of highly technical thermal, breathable and waterproof clothing. The fabrics used are lightweight and often very expensive. These clothes are used for sleeping too, when the explorer climbs into a specially made sleeping bag. Scott's party had none of this. They had to wear layer on layer of sweaters with woollen hats and woollen and fur mittens. Nature provided them with reindeer fur for boots and sleeping bags.

How on earth do you get to the South Pole?

With great difficulty. Even almost a hundred years later, explorers who attempt to make the South Pole on foot are often thwarted by dangerous conditions, even though they have lightweight equipment and sometimes use teams of dogs to help with the load. Imagine what it must have been like for Scott and his party. They did not have the luxury of a dog team and chose to pull their own supplies across the icy wastes of Antarctica.

So what did Scott find at the South Pole?

The following words were recorded in Scott's diary: 'Great God! This is an awful place …' Unfortunately for Scott it was not just the place itself that was awful. As his team approached the Pole they saw a speck in the distance. They got closer and realised the terrible truth – the speck was a Norwegian flag. Roald Amundsen had beaten them to the South Pole and the tracks of his dogs still lay in the snow. All Scott had to show for the journey were diary entries, photographs and 15 kilograms of fossils collected along the way.

What did Scott do next?

All he could do was turn around and lead his party back home. Luck was not on their side, however. They managed to get themselves just a few miles from relative safety but a huge blizzard and frost-bitten limbs prevented them going further. Scott wrote a final entry in his diary on 29 March, 1912 saying: 'The end cannot be far.' Somehow, although on the verge of death, he still managed to write letters to his loved ones. The bodies of the party were found eight months later.

Now write six questions that you would ask Scott in an interview if he were alive today. An example has been done for you. **(6 marks)**

Question: *How did it feel to be only 13 years old and joining the navy?*

Question 1: ....

....

Question 2: ....

....

Question 3: ....

....

Question 4: ....

....

Question 5: ....

....

Question 6: ....

....

Ask open, not closed, questions to get the most out of your interviewee.

Top tip!

Total ── 6

Reading comprehension

1 Read the poem then answer the questions below.

> **Mushrooms by Sylvia Plath**
>
> Overnight, very
> Whitely, discreetly,
> Very quietly
>
> Our toes, our noses
> Take hold on the loam,
> Acquire the air.
>
> Nobody sees us,
> Stops us, betrays us;
> The small grains make room.
>
> Soft fists insist on
> Heaving the needles,
> The leafy bedding,
>
> Even the paving.
> Our hammers, our rams,
> Earless and eyeless,
>
> Perfectly voiceless,
> Widen the crannies,
> Shoulder through holes. We
>
> Diet on water,
> On crumbs of shadow,
> Bland-mannered, asking
>
> Little or nothing.
> So many of us!
> So many of us!
>
> We are shelves, we are
> Tables, we are meek,
> We are edible,
>
> Nudgers and shovers
> In spite of ourselves.
> Our kind multiplies:
>
> We shall by morning
> Inherit the earth.
> Our foot's in the door.

a. From whose point of view is the poem narrated? **(1 mark)**

....

b. Match the following phrases from the poem on the left to the figurative technique on the right. **(2 marks)**

Our foot's in the door   assonance

heaving the needles   repetition

So many of us!/So many of us!   personification

c. What does 'nudgers and shovers' tell you about the way the mushrooms grow? **(2 marks)**

....

....

d. Explain why the poet has used the metaphor 'shelves' and 'tables'.

(1 mark)

....

2 Read the text about Roald Amundsen then answer the questions below.

Roald Amundsen, a Norwegian, spent almost all his adult life in exploration. He was the first explorer to navigate the Northwest Passage between the Atlantic and the Pacific oceans to the north of Canada. However, he is most famous for being the first person to reach the South Pole. Yet his journey to Antarctica was almost an accident.

Amundsen was 37 years old when he decided in 1909 to make an attempt on the North Pole, which had not then been reached. But, while he was preparing for the journey, news came that the American explorer Robert Peary had arrived at the Pole. Amundsen secretly changed his plans, telling only his brother, and headed for the South Pole instead. He knew that a British expedition led by Robert Falcon Scott had already set out with the same aim but, travelling by a different route, he overtook the British party. Amundsen's five-man group set out from his base camp in October 1911 on sledges drawn by huskies on what was to be an eight-week journey. On 14 December 1911, Amundsen reached the Pole and planted the Norwegian flag there. He was about four weeks ahead of Scott.

a. Why did Amundsen decide to head for the South Pole? **(1 mark)**

....

....

b. Why do you think Amundsen kept his plans secret? **(1 mark)**

....

....

c. Explain why you think Amundsen took a different route to Scott. **(1 mark)**

....

d. Why was Amundsen's journey to Antarctica 'almost an accident'?

(2 marks)

....

....

1 Underline the **fronted adverbial** in this sentence. **(1 mark)**

Cautiously, the girls crept into the garden, treading carefully as they went.

2 Replace the underlined word in each sentence with the correct **pronoun. (1 mark)**

When Sonia arrived at her dad's bedside, <u>Sonia</u> could see that he had improved. There was a chair next to the bed and Sonia sat in <u>the chair</u>.

3 Place each underlined word in the correct column in the table. **(1 mark)**

Phil studied the <u>detailed</u> <u>map</u> then put it back neatly in his <u>waterproof</u> <u>rucksack</u>.

Adjective	Noun
....	....
....	....

4 Replace the underlined words in the sentence below with their expanded forms. **(1 mark)**

 <u>I've</u> always loved the end of the summer term when the <u>weather's</u> sunny and <u>we've</u> finished our exams.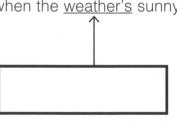

5 What is the function of the sentence below? Tick **one**. **(1 mark)**

What a fuss you have made about nothing!

a question ☐

a command ☐

an exclamation ☐

a statement ☐

6 a. What is the name of the punctuation marks on either side of the words <u>the one from America</u> in the sentence below? **(1 mark)**

My cousin – the one from America – is always talking about celebrities.

....

b. What is the name of a different punctuation mark that could be used correctly in the same place? **(1 mark)**

....

7 Underline one **verb** in each sentence that is in the **present tense**.

a. We love to visit the seaside but last year it was a bit of a washout. **(1 mark)**

b. All through the school year we worked hard, but now is the time to relax.
(1 mark)

8 Insert the most suitable **conjunction** to complete this sentence. **(1 mark)**

Hassan played basketball .... he had a sore wrist.

because   although   however   since

9 Add **inverted commas** to this dialogue. **(1 mark)**

Hurry up or you'll be late for school! shouted my mum. It's almost 9 o'clock.

10 Underline the words in this sentence that tell you it is a **question**. **(1 mark)**

"So you think you're going to win the match tomorrow, do you?"

11 a. Circle the word in the sentence that contains an **apostrophe** to indicate a **contraction**. **(1 mark)**

Mum has been waiting for ages for Katie's bus but it's clearly late.

b. Circle the word in the sentence that contains an **apostrophe** for **possession**. **(1 mark)**

We're thrilled that Jake's birthday celebration wasn't ruined by the bad weather.

12 Insert a pair of commas to indicate **parenthesis** in the sentence below. **(1 mark)**

The family we met on holiday all of whom were very pleasant contacted us last week.

13 Add a **colon** to the sentence below. **(1 mark)**

When I pack for a weekend away in the countryside, I take lots of warm clothes sweaters, boots, gloves and a waterproof coat.

14 Complete the sentence using the **present perfect** form of the verb **to eat**.

(1 mark)

Now that we .... our breakfast, we can set off on our journey.

15 Which event is the **most likely** to happen? Tick **one.** **(1 mark)**

I will finish my homework project this evening. ☐

The forecaster said that it could snow later on. ☐

I might drop your book off at around 9 o'clock. ☐

We may go swimming on Saturday. ☐

16 Underline the **subordinate clause** in the sentence below. **(1 mark)**

My brother went to school today, even though he wasn't feeling well.

17 Put one letter in each box to show what type of word each one is. **(1 mark)**

| **A** (noun) | **B** (adverb) | **C** (verb) | **D** (adjective) |

Mrs Courtney's antique vase suddenly tipped over.

↑ ↑ ↑ ↑
☐ ☐ ☐ ☐

18 Tick the word that is a **synonym** for **mishap**. Tick **one.** **(1 mark)**

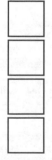

unhappiness

accident

distortion

trick

19 Underline the **two** words in the passage below that show a **command**. **(1 mark)**

Turn to the next page and read the first two paragraphs. What do you think made Theo react that way?

Active voice – The subject of the sentence is doing or being; the object is having it done to them/it

Adjective – A word that describes a noun

Adverb – A word that tells us more about a verb (how, where, when), an adjective, another adverb or a whole clause

Adverbial – A word, phrase or clause that tells us more about a verb (how, where, when) or clause

Alliteration – Repetition of the initial letters of words next to or close to each other

Apostrophe – A punctuation mark used to show omission (contraction) or possession

Assonance – Repetition of vowel sounds inside words

Bias – Supporting one point of view over another

Blurb – A brief overview of the book

Body language – Using your body to get your point across or get the audience's attention

Brackets – Can show parenthesis

By-line – Tells the reader the name of the person who has written the report

Caption – Short description under a picture to explain what it is

Chronological – In the order that something happens

Cohesion – When your whole piece of writing fits together clearly so that it makes sense

Command – A sentence that gives an instruction

Command verb – A verb used to give a command

Commas – Can show parenthesis

Common nouns – Nouns for people, animals and objects

Comprehension – Understanding

Conjunction – Links two words, phrases or clauses

Contraction – A word that has been made shorter

Coordinating conjunction – Links two words, phrases or clauses of equal importance

Dashes – Can show parenthesis

Determiner – A word that introduces a noun such as 'the', 'a', 'some' and 'those'

Direct speech – A sentence in inverted commas showing the exact words spoken by someone

Emotive language – Emotional language used to express feelings

Empathise – To understand and share the feelings of someone else

Emphasis – Stress

Exclamation – A sentence that shows feelings like fear, anger, happiness or excitement

Expanded noun phrase – A phrase with a noun as its main word with other words that tell us more about that noun

Fact – A piece of information that is true

Fiction – Made-up stories

Figurative language – The descriptive language used to create imagery

Fronted adverbial – An adverb or adverbial coming at the start of a sentence

Genre – Type or kind of writing

Gesticulate – To use gestures to emphasise your point

Homophones – Words that sound the same but have different spellings and different meanings

Hook – In this context, it's what grabs the reader's attention (think of a fish grabbing onto a hook on a fishing rod)

Imagery – The use of figurative language to help the reader visualise what is being described

Infer – To form an opinion about something based on the information given rather than from an explicit statement

Informal speech – Relaxed, chatty way of speaking and writing used with family and friends

Inverted commas – The punctuation at the start and end of speech

Main clause – A clause that can make sense as a sentence

Metaphor – A comparison between two things, where the object that is being compared actually is the thing it's compared to

Modal verbs – Verbs that show possibility or likelihood

Non-fiction – Factual information

Noun phrase – A phrase where a noun is the main word

Nouns – Naming words for people, places, animals and things

Onomatopoeia – Words that sound like the thing they are describing

Opinion – What you personally think about something

Parentheses – The punctuation marks used to indicate parenthesis.

Parenthesis – A word or phrase inserted into a sentence as an explanation or afterthought

Passive voice – When the subject isn't carrying out the action but is being acted upon by someone or something

Past – A verb tense showing what has happened

Past perfect – A verb tense formed from the past tense of the verb 'have' + the past participle of the main verb

Past progressive – A verb tense showing a continuous action in the past

Personification – Giving human characteristics to a non-human thing

Possession – Ownership

Possessive determiner – A determiner showing ownership of the noun that immediately follows

Possessive pronoun – A word to show ownership

Prefix – A string of letters added to the start of a word to change its meaning

Preposition – Shows the relationship between the noun or pronoun and other words in the clause or sentence

Present – A verb tense showing what is happening now

Present perfect – A verb tense formed from the present tense of the verb 'have' + the past participle of the main verb

Present progressive – A verb tense showing a continuous action in the present

Pronoun – A word that replaces a noun

Proofreading – Checking your writing for errors and ways to improve it

Proper nouns – Nouns that name particular things. They begin with a capital letter

Pun – A type of word play where the word can have more than one meaning

Question – A sentence that asks something

Quote – Direct speech by a source or witness

Recount – Report retelling an event that has happened

Relative pronoun – The words 'who', 'which', 'that' and 'whose', which introduce a relative clause

Rhetorical question – A question used for effect and with no answer expected

Root word – A word in its own right, without a prefix or a suffix

Scan – A quick reading technique to help you find specific words, phrases and clauses in a text

Silent letter – A letter that was once pronounced but now isn't

Simile – A comparison of two things with similar characteristics

Skim read – A quick reading technique to help you get the gist (the main idea) of a text

Slang – Very informal language used when speaking to friends

Source – Someone who gives the journalist information about the events being reported

Statement – A sentence that gives information

Stress – When you either increase the vowel length or loudness of the syllable, or both

Subordinate clause – A clause which depends on the main clause to make sense

Subordinating conjunction – Joins a subordinate clause to a main clause

Suffix – A letter or a string of letters added to the root word to change or add to its meaning

Syllable – A single, unbroken sound including at least one vowel (or y)

Verb – A word for an action or state of being